# MASCOT® BOOKS

**www.mascotbooks.com**

**For more information, please contact:**
Mascot Books
620 Herndon Parkway #320
Herndon, VA 20170
info@mascotbooks.com

Library of Congress Control Number: 2019911997

CPSIA Code: PRFRE1119A
ISBN-13: 978-1-64543-123-7

Printed in Canada

To Lindsey, Taci, Joshua, Avery, Landon, Emersyn, and
my leading man, Conner, LYM.

# MiRROR MiRROR
## ConFessions oF a Celebrity Makeup Artist

### tRista JORdaN

# Contents

# Introduction

It happened again, my nightmare.

I'm a circus performer balanced on a tightrope above a lion's pen. I lose my footing and fall until I'm face to face with the lion, and I'm mauled. As my limbs are eaten, my body jolts and shoots me straight out of my skin...and my bed.

I don't need to consult a dream expert to interpret what the dream meant. You see, I ran away from a circus—the chaos of my childhood—and ran to join another circus: the movie business. I learned to balance parenthood with a demanding career, and the lion... well...that was the "Harvey Weinsteins" and other toothy challenges I encountered along the way.

I've been journaling my experiences since my first job in Hollywood.

I remember it all like it was yesterday.

I was desperately in need of employment, being a college dropout and single mama with two babies and no family to lean on. Every other job had been a bust, including the time I was hired by a company to untangle their books. I figured out they were in the red and couldn't afford to pay me. That's when I started my own company.

Working for myself was the ticket.

I couldn't afford the day care I'd need to work for someone else, and I could be my own bookkeeper, even though that wasn't necessary. I had 20 bucks to manage and it was tucked in my wallet. I sought out people with money, like lawyers and doctors, and did their grocery shopping, bought birthday gifts plus whatever else they needed, like clothing.

I was a personal Amazon.

I shopped while Lindsey was in school, and Taci I had in tow with me all the time. My last shopping spree ended with a hysterical emergency call: Taci went missing. She had been following me around the umpteenth clothing store and, in an instant, she was gone. She checked out before we went through the checkout.

Well, not really.

She was hiding inside the center of a circular clothing rack; her way of telling me she was done shopping. Forever. So we went home to our dumpy trailer, with a sleeping mattress on the floor and very little food in our mini fridge. As a distraction from our hunger, I introduced my daughters to our first lessons in art.

We colored on the trailer walls.

My next jobs involved dabbling in different entertainment departments, including casting, but nothing resonated. When I landed in makeup—a big step up from my creative crayon lessons—I knew I'd found my home: cleaning brushes, self-teaching, learning the ropes, acquiring technique, watching, practicing, and immersing myself in total gratitude because every day was Take Your Daughter to Work Day.

It didn't happen overnight, but it happened.

Fast-forward three years.

Day one as an official makeup artist, my hands were shaking and my heart was racing. I had my powder brush loaded. I was holding my breath waiting for production to shout the magic words, my prompt to do my thing. A big part of me was hoping they would forget I was there. Would I rather the actress have a shiny nose? Yes, yes I would. Walking in front of the camera and crew members was unnerving...everyone would have their jobs finished. I was the last to complete mine, so all eyes would be on me.

The AD, which stands for assistant director, announced, "Stand by, quiet please."

The lights were set.

The camera was ready to roll.

The actress was ready to deliver her lines.

And I was still waiting.

I paced, shuffled, anxious for my cue.

Finally, it was show time. "Last looks!"

*Oh, dear...oh, no...I'm up.*

I ran in, literally. However, unknowingly, I'd wrapped a power cord around my foot while pacing. So, as I rushed at Mach 4 speed onto the set, the lights, stands, flags, monitor...well, everything fell like a line of dominos. It started with me and ended with the last light setup.

Yep, I took it all down.

Omen?

You could call it that, the shaky start of a career that took me on one hell of a roller-coaster ride.

Since that first day 20 years ago, I've worked on over 50 feature films, dozens of television shows, zillions of commercials, and music videos, most notably the 2015 Macklemore hit "Downtown," which has been watched over 144 million times on YouTube.

Other highlights?

Of course, I'm a makeup and hair stylist—we love highlights!

I've worked with thousands of celebrities, been accused of killing one, and mourned the deaths of a few. I've also been racially profiled for being white, played in the World Series of Poker, and partied with people like Leonardo DiCaprio. I've been involved in criminal activity, staged a murder, and solved a few mysteries. I even "cheated on" my gay hairstylist and put makeup on Mozart. If that's not enough, I've put beach wave hair extensions on a horse, given a dog sutures, and pulled a few rabbits out of hats.

And that's just the beginning.

Everything in this book is true and, when possible, I've used real names. In some instances, I used fake names to protect the innocent and not-so-innocent—and to protect myself because I don't relish the idea of being in a lawsuit.

Ethics are important.

An interesting fact of my world is the silent makeup artist code of ethics. It states, "What goes on inside the makeup trailer, stays in the makeup trailer."

But I ask, is it a cardinal sin to confess the treacherous land mines among which my profession dances?

I think not.

It's time to stand up and speak out.

Everyone else is doing it.

Why not me, too?

# STudenT

At the beginning of my career I was blinded by the bright lights, the glitz, and the glam. I became a student of the business and I was anxious to do well and prove myself, or at the very least just fit in and not get fired.

I was brushing my teeth and washing my face—my nightly ritual while falling asleep standing—when I heard my phone ring.

"I need to give you some notes." The producer for the show was a nice man, maybe a little socially awkward. He smiled too much.

"Okay, in the morning before we start?"

"You mean call time, Trista?"

"Yes, yes, sorry, exactly." I hadn't finished Lingo 101. This wasn't my first show, but, seriously, does "call time" seem like a real reference?

"No, let me swing them over to you now."

I didn't even know what "notes" were. Is this like in school when you pass the note to your friend when the teacher isn't looking? Couldn't he just slip it under my makeup trailer door in the morning, while I was hiding, trying to figure out what my day looked like as I chugged down a gallon of coffee?

I answered the door in my sweats. He started talking without preamble. "When we were doing scene assemblies the editor noticed...first things first...do you have anything to drink?"

"Well, I'm not really...oh, l have beer, wine..." Damn, I will have to brush my teeth again. This must be bad news if the producer thought I needed a drink before he delivered my note—and what the hell is an assembly? In high school an assembly meant fun and no class, but this doesn't sound like either.

"A beer sounds great. I just broke up with my girlfriend; it's been pretty rough. Do you want to watch a movie?" He was lurching from one idea to the next.

"Oh, I'm so sorry, relationships are hard..." I tried to sympathize.

"She actually didn't like the way I kissed...Can you believe that?"

"How silly..." Maybe he just needed a friend to talk to, but I needed sleep before I pretended to be a friend. I had just worked a 16-hour film day.

"I think I need kissing lessons. Let me show you."

Holy Moses, I definitely need him to go, just pass the note—I think the school bell is about to ring. I was paralyzed in fear. I didn't want to be rude. My father threw coffee cups if you even looked at him sideways—which I never did. Instead, I watched my sister get nailed.

"Ya know, I'm really tired..." He leaned in and planted one, as I stood frozen with my hands glued to my sides. I knew friends don't kiss like that. I was confused...did he want to date me? Producers, friends, huh?

"Gee, I think I drank too much, Trista...Excuse me for a moment..."

Well, that explains everything. He can leave after he uses the bathroom. He must have drunk before he arrived, because only half his beer was gone. He can just forget this happened if indeed he's intoxicated, but he didn't appear to be so. I heard the bathroom door open and I was relieved the uncomfortable situation was ending.

"I'm not able to drive...I will have to spend the night," he declared, and he headed to my bedroom in his tighty-whities, which blended into his milky white skin.

I didn't want to hurt his feelings, or for him to think I didn't like him, but I no longer liked him. I had months to go before that film would wrap. Was this a condition for my employment? Was this a test? I always did do well on tests. I went to school.

I quickly slipped onto the edge of my bed and rolled onto my side, facing away from him and crossed my arms in an X.

I never join men in bed so easily...but he's my boss.

*I lie frozen.*

The lion moved closer.

A tear escaped and rolled down onto my pillowcase.

His body touched mine.

I exhaled slowly out my nose and intentionally made a soft snoring noise, acting as if I was in a deep sleep.

As he lay next to me I felt his enemy hardening. I focused on my fake sleeping breath and I was no longer present, as if I had left my body and a barrier had formed.

After what seemed to be hours, but was really only minutes, he moved to the other side of the bed.

Sometimes, cheating on tests is necessary.

I was thankful I dodged a fatal bullet, but I lived in a foggy hazed cloud for several weeks asking myself, what did I do wrong to put myself in a vulnerable situation? If I had asked him to leave would I still have a job? Why couldn't I say something? If I did, would I be pegged as a "troublemaker?"

I was applying makeup on my actor when I heard the lion's voice.

The friendly producer had entered my trailer. I hadn't seen him since my sleepless night of frozen terror. I felt perspiration...not under my arms or my forehead, but on my legs. I'm always cool as a cucumber even on the hottest of summer days like that one. It was my own pee, dribbling down my legs. I knew I was permanently damaged, and when night fell, I had my first nightmare. It took me a lifetime before I could wear shorts again, and I still sleep with my arms crossed.

# Puzzle Solver

My primary job is as a professional makeup artist. I know it might seem like a frivolous occupation, however, I'm also called on to fulfill dozens of different responsibilities, and deciphering the psychological puzzle pieces is most definitely the uppermost on the list. I have to think quickly on my feet and deal with lots of unexpected crazy situations.

Christina Ricci was a child actress in the '90s when she starred in *The Addams Family* and since then, she has had prominent roles opposite Charlize Theron in *Monster*, Samuel L. Jackson in *Black Snake Moan*, and Johnny Depp in *Sleepy Hollow*. I was excited to meet an actress I'd long admired for both her uniqueness and the high-level mastery of her craft.

Ms. Ricci entered the trailer with her traveling girlfriend and promptly slid aside the displayed makeup boxes I had researched specifically for her. She replaced my organized, new, unopened choices with the contents from inside her bag, along with her Diet Coke and a bag of chips, and she declared, "I don't know much about anything, Trista, but what I do know is that I'm an expert on makeup." Well, I always liked a straight shooter.

I picked through her cosmetic bag, looking for the best place to start and quickly realized this job was going to be miserable. Her Chanel foundation was very dry and all her colors appeared to be very old. I was sure I could skip my standard pre-question, "Do you have any sensitivities I should be aware of?" Clearly she was good to go if she wore a Petri dish of bacteria.

Christina slid into the makeup chair and closed her eyes. A female guest for another actress sat at the adjacent station in the chair closest to us, with bugged-out doe eyes, not at all interested in my chemistry skills with the unforgiving crappy makeup I spilled out from Christina's makeup bag. No, her eyes were glued to me. She was examining me as if my shirt were see-through, and when our eyes met she slowly licked her little finger and brought it to her lap. I threw a little shade. She can make gestures to the back of my head. I started sneaking and mixing in a little of my aloe, my favorite oil-free moisturizer, so I could work Christina's un-moveable foundation onto her skin. If we'd had a camera test, weeks before, we would've worked it out. I would be far more prepared...for the makeup—not the company.

Years earlier, I did makeup for a pre-*The Mentalist* and *The Fix* Robin Tunney. She insisted on meeting me during pre-production at her house in Griffith Park, Los Angeles. We did a run-through on her makeup weeks before shooting the movie. It meant less stress on both of us. I could've bought Christina some new Chanel, if only we had done a makeup test before day one of shooting, but my request to do a pre-production trial had been denied.

My first scene with Christina Ricci was at the airport, out on the tarmac. Special badges were issued for crew members working in the high clearance area. Lighting, camera rehearsals, and blocking had all been completed before my arrival to set. My first order of business was to find my perch: an out-of-the-way cubby that was close to set, behind the camera, clear of lights, with an eyeshot of talent, view of the monitor, and ability to hear the director. Oh, and a table would be great for easy access to my kits, and it would be useful if there were room for my assistants and the hairstylists on my perch. Note to producers: you might want to build makeup artists their own sets, and one for yourselves, for that matter. Most of the movie producers I know are either on the phone talking obliviously while we are filming...or entering a closed set...or sitting behind the monitor, which is prime real estate for crew members (like myself) who need to see what's going on. So, a movie producer equals annoyances.

I reviewed the "sides" for details on the next scene up (the sides are a mini version of the script for the scenes shot that day) and turned my phone to silent. Those wave interference hits can cause the soundman to turn *un*-silent. I loaded my brushes with product and placed them into my apron to shave minutes off of the time it takes to do last looks. The searching and digging inside the kits for brushes and makeup would've been time consuming. We were about to partake in a bull charge and every second counted. I was the key lead on this film, so I met with my other artists in my department and gave them last-minute instructions. Each assistant artist and hairstylist had their own actors on whom to do finishing touches. I assigned the cast members an artist based on needs and timing. There are circumstances when we each have numerous cast members for whom we're responsible.

The next scene up was coverage on Christina. The camera and director's focus would be on her. This is when the endless possibilities of what my actor will need from me become a riddle. At times I'm still a student needing answers. Did she treat herself to another bag of chips and eat her lipstick off? Does she look shiny and will she need a puff of powder? Is she too matte and needs a little contour? Are the colors I chose earlier still working or did she do a last-minute wardrobe change? What does she look like in this outdoor lighting versus inside the makeup trailer? What will need to be adjusted? Hell, there are a million puzzle pieces that need to fit. These thoughts make me apprehensive. I don't want to slow down production. I have zero experience with Christina's skin, and her personality. We had just met when she walked into the trailer.

If—and this is a big highly unlikely if—nothing on my actor's face needs changing, I will shout out, "Makeup is clear!" Those three words are magic. There's no touching or taking any time from the camera department breathing fire to shoot. I'm always hopeful an actor's makeup still looks as fresh as it did in the makeup trailer, but it's one enormous if.

But even a pre-production run-through like the one I did for Robin Tunney doesn't mean unexpected situations can't arise. The Tunney project was shooting in a hotel and while we were waiting for a new scene to be set up, Robin slipped into a room away from the set for a little siesta. Would you sleep on your made-up face? Or perhaps, and this is just a suggestion, would you sleep face-up? Protecting the makeup I spent time and talent applying? Just asking, because you know where I'm going with this? When Robin entered the set and "Last looks!" was called, she had a distinct, deep pillow seam line imprinted from her forehead, down through both eyes and down the chin. Why yes, people, it's not easy to remember your face is primed with my makeup application and ready for "action!" What's an artist to do? I can't fix stupid, but as a puzzle solver, I can try. I have a front-row seat on lots of colorful pieces.

But this was still my first day with Ms. Ricci. Time will tell. What conundrums would unfold? The directors were giving me the look. The look that says, "Shouldn't you know where Christina is?" Okay, that's not my job. The second-second (assistant director to the first assistant) should have the eagle eye on talent and know exactly where they are at all times, even during the days off-camera. After all, actors are considered precious commodities. Those two-way radios everyone wears like a fashionable accessory are buzzing with the search, which has officially started. Somehow, some way, Christina has eluded the directing staff. What is her "20" (movie lingo for "state your location")? Has she hidden? I was in kindergarten when I learned to hide. It started when I fell asleep during quiet time and the teacher had a hard time waking me. She ridiculed me while the class laughed. They didn't know I was up all night listening to my parents arguing. I walked myself to school, so it was easy to slip into the church and wait for the sounds of kids walking home. Attendance wasn't a thing when I was six, but it is during movie making.

Shortly after the search began, out popped Christina Ricci, ready and willing to shoot. I had no spectacular issues with her makeup except the knowledge that my cosmetic choices would've looked fresher. I took a picture after the first take; it's standard protocol to match the continuity for future scenes. Storylines are not filmed in chronological order. We shoot within each location. I refer to my pictures with the scene number to match her look on a future date. When she changes wardrobes for a different day in the story, I will change her makeup and then take a picture for when we shoot days or weeks later, so it doesn't become a brainteaser to match the makeup. Continuity is extremely important.

Not only am I responsible for the way actors look on camera, but I also have a pivotal role in how they feel. The quicker I can assess the psychological warfare I'm dealing with, the less bumpy the project ride is going to be. This is a crucial piece to my puzzle.

I filmed with Academy Award winning actor Cuba Gooding Jr. on several movies. My absolute favorite character he played was the football player who said, "Show me the money" in *Jerry McGuire*.

Cuba has a fear of the number six. If I ended my makeup brush stroke on the number six or any combination of sixes, such as 12, 18, or 24, he would open his eyes in total fear until I touched him again, landing on a seven or any number *not* divisible by six. I developed a new technique...the "*cubaconfusa,*" and you can find the "Tristinary" in the back of the book.

I smudged quickly and in different directions without lifting my brush so it was virtually impossible to count. I could see his closed eyes fluttering, pulsing, trying to impossibly add numbers and catch up with the rubbing. I knew I was messing with him, but it was all in fun. He never knew.

Christina constantly disappeared on set. I was convinced this was a hint of evidence to solving her psychological puzzle. She doesn't eat much. Does she have a closeted sweet tooth, and I need to keep Skittles on hand? Maybe she's at church?

Day three, she slid into my makeup chair for her application. "Trista, what do you think of the makeup I gave you?"

Was this a trick question? Was she giving me permission really to speak my mind? As a puzzle solver I tread cautiously. "Well, Christina, I'm happy to continue using your makeup." Sometimes lying is completely necessary in this business. Me not dumb. "However, if you are open to a change, I can try some other options."

On the first day, she had made such a big deal for me to use her own stuff. Now, she gave me the affirmative nod to bring out my wares. She closed her eyes and I got busy. When I finished, she left promptly with not even one glance at her reflection. On occasion I have actors who will go to their own trailer and do a critical study in a magnified mirror, only to quickly return with minute corrections and further discussions. This did not happen with Christina. I felt I had turned an important corner, but I still felt a shroud of mystery.

After her next scene, I did my customary routine and took a continuity photo. I compared it to pictures using her personal makeup and I saw a remarkable difference when I used mine. Her overall appearance was more polished, blended, and brighter. I was excited to share it with Christina.

Day four, I prepared for Ms. Ricci's shower scene, where she would be wearing only a towel. We used a special gel product to keep her hair looking wet, along with Evian water to spray her down. When she sat down in the makeup chair, a few of my continuity photos were in front of her. Christina became extremely agitated. "Trista, I don't ever want to see photos of me. I don't like seeing myself in the mirror. I especially don't like my pictures. I would've said something sooner, but I'm super shy."

I was blindsided by her disclosure. I'd had the wrong inklings. Looking back on the previous few days, I realized she'd always kept her eyes closed and left the trailer promptly. She never asked for a hand mirror to check before a close-up on set. She was always distancing herself from cast and crew. Hmm...there were several missed hints that should've been my "aha" moments to unravel the psychological mystery.

Just when I was wrestling with Christina's issues and how to deal with them, Irwin Winkler, the director, took me aside. I always found Mr. Winkler to be a browbeater. He reminded me of my father. However, I have immense respect for him—Mr. Winkler, not my father. He's an Academy Award winning producer for *Rocky*, along with getting Oscar nods for *Goodfellas* and *Raging Bull*. He has a long list of extremely successful films.

"Christina has lots of tattoos. 'Sarah,' her character, wouldn't. Get rid of them. Now," Winkler snapped curtly, while my stomach turned into mush.

Shooting call was in five minutes. Giddy-up. The last time Irwin demanded my attention was in a scene at the makeshift Walter Reed Army Medical Center. I filmed with Jessica Biel and he wanted shrapnel wounds on one side of her face. She played a soldier who had been seriously injured when her Humvee was bombed. Her character lost her arm in the explosion. These new scars for Jessica were not discussed in any meetings, or listed on the call sheet. Of course it made sense she would have remnants of this accident upon her return home from the tour in the Iraq war. However, time heals all wounds and it's not my place to overthink the script. I whipped out my illustrator pallet and painted, while Winkler watched and interjected. Jess lay on the gurney in front of a camera, which was ready to roll. I felt as if I were lying in front of a Humvee…and it was ready to roll.

But now I understood what Christina needed from me. The puzzle was solved. She was timid and had a phobia with having her self-image publicly displayed. I kept her pictures hidden and used them secretly as a reference. I turned her chair to apply makeup so she wasn't facing the mirror. I did her touch-ups quickly and away from cast and crew. The tattoo cover-ups were tedious. However, I had a newfound understanding and empathy for Christina Ricci.

When "last looks" was broadcast, I paused. Will I be able to say those precious three words: "Makeup is clear?" Will the camera department get their wish? No last-minute surprises, director requests, actor fiascos, or meltdowns? Will I understand the psychological puzzle pieces of my celebrities enough to do my job effectively? I studied Christina. She was beautiful, even if she didn't see her reflection in the mirror. Every pixel. The big *if* happened. The Red Sea parted, the heavens opened, and I'm anointed oh, Holy One. "Makeup is clear."

# Crime Sleuth

Marvin Link had a mission: robbery. He put on a wig, slathered makeup on his face, applied concealing material to prevent fingerprints, grabbed his gun, and was off. Within minutes, the brave men and women in blue who placed him in cold steel bracelets and transported him to free accommodations in the county hotel foiled Link's master plan. This may be the ultimate penalty for wasting perfectly good makeup.

Link also had pending charges on dealing drugs, with several witnesses to testify against him. As a result, Link came up with yet another game plan: vengeance. He begged his cellmate, Abram, to kill the two witnesses. Because Abram was an undercover narcotics agent, the police became aware of the contract hit.

The police developed a game plan of their own. That's where I came in. They hired me to help stage the deaths of those courageous witnesses. We'd fake the mock crime scene of the murdered witnesses; the informant Abram would show the criminal, Link, photographic evidence of his contracted plan; and when he acknowledged approval of the payoff, he'd officially be toast.

Why did they hire me? Well, I had just finished with makeup on three episodes of *Unsolved Mysteries* and I knew it was dead-on when they say, "Life imitates art."

Joe and Barbie, the witnesses, agreed to the ruse. They were scared out of their minds. I was scared for my life and was happy I had another makeup artist to accompany me for this dangerous mission. I agreed to help serve justice with one condition. I insisted and was promised there would be no mention of our involvement.

I was on edge. Our secret sting operation started with the clinical guidance of a forensic pathology specialist. The pathologist asked if I could make an air-mucus bubble appear from the nostril of our make-believe murdered witnesses. I've had bizarre requests before, but really?

The cause of death would be a gunshot wound. The expert explained the bullet's velocity, noting the entry would be markedly smaller and more symmetrical when compared to the exit wound, which would be larger, more irregular, and torn.

The caliber of the gun used determined the size of the bullet holes. Another factor was the standing distance of the shot. A gun fired in direct contact with the skin, which was the case here, caused particles of burning and unburned powder to become embedded in the skin, which can't be wiped away and create what's known as "tattooing"—an abrasion ring.

To build the execution-style holes on the face of one of the witnesses, I used mortician's wax. It seemed darker and more eerie than usual on that hot August night. Where were the stars and the moon? The wax wouldn't stay up and kept sliding from Barbie's face, but then again she was sweating "bullets" from her pores. I used ice on the back of her neck to keep her cool. We drove to a wooded area and actually rolled Joe and Barbie down a remote hill, for authenticity. After they landed safely at the bottom, I used my dirt kit. Yes, I buy dirt. It comes in different colors and in big canisters: oil can greasy, grime, from light to dark, wet and dry. Actually, isn't all makeup dirt? It's just a wide range of substances and pigments. I've used lipstick to make a bruise, blush to make an eye shadow, and dark brown eye shadows to make smudges. If I didn't have a dirt makeup kit, I'm sure I could've cooked up something as a substitute. I applied dark, dry, smudgy dirt powder to Joe and Barbie's skin and clothes, as dark would best replicate the sinister scene to be photographed. I also had an inventory of blood types, pigments, and flavors. My favorites are peppermint for yummy tasting mouth blood and gooey gels for scabs. For this murder application I poured dark blue blood from the bullet holes to drip in the direction of the fall. Ten minutes elapsed between the staged shooting and pictures, so no extra effects were needed for postmortem changes. If additional changes were necessary, I was ready with my skin illustrator paint pallet, in green for discoloration to mimic decomposition.

The big moment happened. It was time to make or break this master plan of perception versus reality. Yep, it was do or die time. We had Joe and Barbie hold their breath. It worked in film, why wouldn't it translate onto Polaroid? We directed Barbie to keep her eyes open (doll eyes) and Joe to keep his closed, an "opposites attract" artwork. The detectives clicked the important simulated homicidal photos.

The next phase of this undercover sting operation was to prove Marvin Link had taken a substantial step toward the commission of a criminal act and intended to solicit another to kill Joe and Barbie to prevent them from testifying against him.

Joe and Barbie were hidden at a hotel immediately following their staged fake murders. It was crucial they stay concealed from anyone who knew Marvin Link until the "proof of death" photographs could be shown to him.

Link closely examined the gruesome images of death during the next jailhouse visit with Abram, the undercover narc. He approved the payoff. Boom. Bang. Busted.

The police filed new charges against Link, but did not make public the names of the informant or the two witnesses. In fact, they actually documented the witnesses as both being male, sort of like a secret clue no one was aware of except the inner circle. For their future safety, Joe and Barbie were entered into the Federal Witness Protection Program. They had feared revenge from Link or his associates.

On the front page of the Chicago newspaper article the first sentence read, "Police hired a makeup artist to make two men [as you know one was actually a woman] appear to be shot to death." I'd like to know what happened to the promise made to us. Our names were not mentioned, but I wondered about our safety. My makeup partner moved away, and I followed.

Marvin Link was convicted and sentenced to serve oodles of years in prison for conspiracy to commit first-degree robbery, possession of a firearm, and a contract hire to kill. He was also designated as an armed career criminal.

Ironically, makeup was Link's ultimate demise. He was wearing makeup when he was initially arrested and now with the application of special effects makeup, he could've been the subject of a *Dateline* episode. It's all about dirty makeup...it's a crime.

Years later I was involved in another criminal incident, but it didn't involve blood and bullets. I was in Las Vegas watching my Chicago Blackhawks fight for the Stanley Cup at the bar of Japonais, at the Mirage Casino. They grilled lobster tails for me, dripping with butter and garlic, and I'm on my limit of Cabernet. Umm...am I ever on my limit of Cabernet? I had a flight to catch to meet my call time in the morning and I was cutting it close, but I just had to see my Hawks win.

After Chicago won, I scurried to the airport taxi line, while the bellhop rounded up my luggage. He commented on my "nice" dress. I had bought my white mini with tulip sleeves at the Mirage boutique. It was a necessity; I had run out of clean clothes.

At the airport I rushed to the kiosk to print a boarding pass and the document read, "Security Breach. Not a valid document." I had never seen such a message, so I tried again. Ditto. I only had minutes to reach my gate, so I dashed to the security podium with my driver's license, and surprisingly they let me through along with another gal who was in a similar hurry. She wore a white sundress and her hair was in a high messy bun similar to mine. We both reached the same gate and the attendant displayed a quizzical look on her face. She told us to wait. The plane had already boarded and we were the last two remaining. A security guard escorted us onto the plane and pointed to the last two end seats, opposite each other on the aisle. Another airport security officer came on board and looked at me. "Lisa?"

"No, my name is Trista."

He glared at the other late boarder and she responded, "Bonnie."

"Well, one of you is lying."

I'm confused...maybe I *should* have a limit on Cabernet?

The officer continued. "This plane isn't moving until Lisa gets off."

I reached for my purse and handed over my identification, as did Bonnie.

The officer went to the back of the plane to have a conversation with a gentleman passenger. Bonnie simultaneously slid on her dark sunglasses and grabbed a sweater from her carry-on. The passengers were giving me the stink eye for delaying the flight, and I was giving Bonnie the once-over. A little late to hide her appearance, wasn't it?

The officer made his way toward our seats and focused on Bonnie.

"Lisa, your fake I.D. isn't going to help you here; when we arrive in Spokane the police will be waiting for you. Just make it easy on yourself and deplane. Now."

After what seemed like an eternity, Bonnie/Lisa left in a huff. The flight attendants began their ritual. "If we can have your attention, there are six exits on this…"

While we were in the air, I went into detective mode to investigate the mix-up. Apparently, a passenger had seen his stalker when he entered the airport and immediately called security. He gave them the description of Lisa sporting a "high messy bun" and "wearing a short, white dress." She was a very dangerous woman and a warrant was still pending for her arrest. Security saw us looking the same part, so they shut us both down. Why wasn't my new purchase in Vegas a black dress? That is my favorite go-to color.

When we arrived in Spokane—late—there appeared to be another problem. The door was opened to the jet bridge, but we were not allowed to depart. Oh, my God, was Lisa hiding in the bathroom? I hadn't actually seen her leave. I guessed anything was possible.

My assumption was incorrect. In rushed a medical team to administer emergency treatment to an elderly passenger having a heart attack, and it wasn't the passenger being stalked. Perhaps all the fuss was a contributing factor?

I think the real crime was that it took six months to get me off the no-fly list, and every time I entered an airport I felt like I was having a heart attack. CSI Spokane was a wrap when I was free to fly.

I remember working on a big movie and wishing I had my own wings. Free to fly far, far away with my own personal crime detective to save my day.

I was working with William. He was one of those actors who overthought his makeup.

"This scene requires a clear mascara on my lashes to create the slightest hint of more drama," he explained.

Yeah, right. You're enough drama. He would leave my chair, study himself at his mirror inside his trailer, and then revisit me. After his tenth call for the same scene, I was asked to visit his trailer. I assumed he was tired of making the trip. After I entered, he locked the door. Geez, was it a top-secret makeup request? Did he want invisible freckles to create the illusion of fake boyishness?

"Hey, I guess we have time, lots of it...the director pushed back my scene to the end of the day."

"Time?" I couldn't imagine any makeup application taking much time.

William took off his pants. "You're a *make-out* artist, aren't you?"

I was about to be eaten by a lion, but I froze. He pushed me against the wall, and onto my knees. I wanted to scream, but I couldn't. Then, a miracle: a knock on the door. "Trista, you're wanted on set..."

I exited like a shocked baby Bambi given a second chance to live. I went straight to the producer's office. He was an authoritative man, and I knew he would protect me after I told him what happened.

"Trista, stop wearing your pants so tight," he suggested. I swore I heard my kindergarten class laughing at me.

Did it really matter what I wore...shorts, pants, sweats? If I wear a sleeveless, backless, slit-to-the-navel mini dress does it mean I want to have sex? Can you hear me screaming?

Then there was the film requiring me to use my own keen detective skills to defend myself against accusations of sabotage.

Billy entered the trailer for his makeup test. His main notoriety was from a super iconic movie and he played one of the leads as a very stuffy, not-so-nice love interest; one of those characters you loved to hate.

He brought his personal shaving kit and gave me strict instructions to have it available for him each and every morning. He also gave me harsh guidelines on how to store it, with no access to anyone else. I'm always careful not to cross-contaminate between actors. It's what I do. It's a ritual. Billy's delivery of his information was offensive, but, he didn't know me. I assured him of my safety routines and clearly labeled a visible space "Billy."

On this particular movie, my trailer wasn't the typical one. It wasn't customized with several makeup and hair stations. No, this was a little tin can set up to sleep in, actually. There was one shelving area, a tiny workspace, one mirror, a director's chair, and at the other end a living area and small kitchenette. Billy had another project he had to finish during the time we were filming ours. He was scheduled to fly to another location and return a week later. We continued to work around his schedule. This overlapping of projects sometimes happens. It's hard to match up cast members who have a similar block of time. While Bernie, the driver, was waiting to transport Billy to the airport, he rushed in and grabbed his shaving kit to take with him to the other film he was working on. A peace-filled week without Billy and his precious shaving kit. Oh, yeah!

When he returned from the other filming project, Billy asked, "Trista, where's my shaving kit?"

"I gave it to you before you left so you could take it with you, remember?" I prompted Billy while his eyes flared. My head started to hurt.

"No, I don't have it. I had to use some other dumbass electric razor the other makeup department had on hand."

"I'm so sorry, Billy. I will have the production assistant purchase you a replacement."

"No, I need mine. The one I left with you. Where did you put it?"

Amy, my adorable BFF "sisteress," who is also my makeup assistant, followed me around and kept my life organized. I'm known to leave a trail, especially when it comes to my keys. Amy had made a labeled pocket on the top right side of my large makeup drawers just for my car keys because she knows me so well. However, I knew what I knew, and so did Amy. I didn't misplace his shaver the way I do my keys. I did a ceremonious passing of his precious goods like a sacred baton hand-off in an Olympic relay race.

Amy and I called a search party for the missing black bag. If he didn't have it on his last location and it wasn't in the makeup trailer, well then, people...on your mark, get set, go. The hunt was on. I'm sure it would have been cheaper to go to the store and purchase a new one. This was a shaver, not his grandfather's rare and irreplaceable pocket watch.

We were asking my tribe to leave their regular production jobs to do a search and rescue mission. This was like one of those word math problems. If you have 10 people and they each get paid so many peanuts per hour and you ask each one to go on a treasure hunt for X number, how many peanuts have you lost? It was nuts.

Billy went to the producer and accused me of grave negligence. I was beginning to think this was a case of sabotage. Perhaps we call this "Shave-gate" and Billy votes to have me impeached and my successor will preside over the department.

It was the second day after Billy's return and no shaver. He had to use mine, to keep his beard scruff continuity correct. It annoyed him, but pictures don't lie, and he looked the same. Whew. It was more painful for me worrying about his reaction.

I decided to take matters into my own hands. Sherlock Holmes, at your service. After everyone wrapped up for the day and the transportation department was cleaning the basecamp trailers, I snuck into Billy's trailer. I went through every nook, top to bottom. I took special care not to disturb anything. If a drawer was half-open, I kept it half-open. Perhaps I really could be a detective?

Nope. Nothing. He must have taken it with him to the other location, but he was so damn convinced I had it. Well, he's an actor... and a damn good one.

I returned to my trailer and gathered my belongings. I started hoofing the long walk to the parking area, but Bernie the transpo-driver offered to drive me. I jumped in the back and tossed my purse to my feet. "Thanks, Bernie." He pulled up to the only car left in the lot as I grabbed my purse—it was stuck on a black bag under the seat.

"Bernie, Bernie...this is incredible!" I held up Billy's shaving kit as if I was showcasing a trophy. "Shave-gate" was now in the history books.

Sometimes it's necessary to prevent a crime. Natalie, my friend's daughter, was working a show as a video assistant. My actor (who was 30 years her senior) showered her with compliments and flirted nonstop. Then, the big ask: "I just talked to my producer and they need you on my next film. I can take care of your travel expenses and lodging." I was on the phone talking to Natalie's mama faster than you can say "not on my watch." My next call was to a doctor. I started therapy.

I recall another crime-solving mission when I worked on a project with a spider wrangler. The subjects were African wolf spiders... those big, creepy, hairy ones. This is the cue for those with arachnophobia to skip ahead a few pages. Warning served.

I can't believe those creatures actually have a purpose. What is their role in life besides grossing us out? There were 175 cages. None of the wolves sported matching numbers on their backs, but the numbered cages were used to account for each one as they were ushered individually into their cells. They should be prison cells, locked up forever with no parole.

I was standing next to Nigel, the soundman from England, using his monitor to watch my actors, when the A.D. called "lunch." I loved saying his name: Nigh-gel. We playfully bantered in his native English dialect—his authentic, mine pitiful. "I'm feeling a bit peckish for nosh, Trista."

We had completed the scene with the spiders and the wrangler was using a big handheld air mover to retreat them back to their cages. Nigel and I were ready for "nosh" when the wrangler broadcasted that we had an empty cage. "Everyone hold still, one hairy eight-legger is missing."

"Bring out the hoover, Trista looks bloody dauncy." Nigel looked down at my bare toes in flip-flops. "You should be wearing 'Wellie boots.'"

This was before I paid attention to OSHA rules stating closed-toe shoes are a must around heavy equipment, or spiders. I suddenly skipped my desire to be a crime sleuth—no need. Everyone on set played a game of statue while the wrangler searched for the missing spider. I, however, wanted to play a different game. The hell with statue; let's play tag and I plan to run away, with no worries I would step on number 35 while I hightail it to the exit. If I continued to stand there and play statue, the beast would single me out and bite off all my toes, I'm sure of it. Then they will need to call a medi-helicopter to airlift me to the hospital. Did they call to make sure anti-wolf-spider venom was on hand? Be careful what you think because you can be a magnet to your worries...

"*Aaaaaaauugh!*" I screamed. Number 35 landed on me. It crawled slowly up my mid-back toward my shoulders. Should I fight or flight from the fright? Would it fly off me if I ran for it, because air seemed to be its nemesis, or do I drop and roll? No, that's the action during a fire, but it felt like an earthquake, because my world was shaking. The decision was an easy one, because, well, I *couldn't* move. The statue game won me over. Everyone broke his or her mannequin poses and came running to my original game. I was tagged, "You're it." My only consolation was to regain my coveted title as a crime solver if I captured the hairy beast.

"I found him," the wrangler shouted from the opposite part of the room.

"My mistake, Trista, oh, my *gawd!*" Nigel had done a boyish prank where he fluttered his fingers up my back. This was just a little crime story about the makeup artist who cried wolf.

I did, however, choose to be a crime solver earlier in my career, when I helped one of my friends. She had entered a local beauty pageant and discovered they were looking for a makeup artist to help with the staged event. Unlike in the movies, I had no call sheet with a schedule of who would be in my chair, and there was no character development in the script. It was just a long line of women playing the same role of "I've got to win."

Many elements of the makeup application were different from those of filming. These Washington contestants had judges in the front row who they were obviously trying to impress; they had an audience needing to see them from a distance; the lighting was insanely bright; and they'd be changing their wardrobe several times during the course of the show. This was a perplexing dilemma. What's an artist to do? I fumbled my way through it and it landed me future employment.

The pageant system hired me to continue at a national level. They booked my flight and instructed me to take a shuttle when I landed in Houston.

When I arrived, I handed the address to the shuttle driver. "Ma'am, this is going to be expensive. Let me call dispatch and ask about traveling this far."

"What do you mean?" I stopped fussing with my luggage.

"Plano, Texas is on the other side of the state, closer to Dallas."

I immediately turned around and searched for a phone. This was back in the late '90s. Cell phones weren't prevalent, so when I say phone I mean the nearest working pay phone. The pageant's travel coordinator apologized for booking me incorrectly.

As my plane sat on the tarmac, waiting for my departure to Dallas from Houston, smoke billowed inside the cabin. We were evacuated back into the airport. I retreated and repeated, waiting for another plane to be sent, and the search to find another pay phone ensued. The travel coordinator arranged to have a car waiting for me upon arrival in Dallas. Time was of the essence and I already had signifi-cant delays for that evening's event.

I let out a sigh of relief when I finally reached my seat on the re-placement plane. I have two speeds: go and stop. Sitting makes me stop...kind of like hitting a wall. While the stewardess—that's what we called them back in the dark ages—was going through take-off rituals, I fell into a deep sleep.

When I woke up, I didn't hear the hum of the engines. Oh, Lord, help me. What's happening? I stood up and shouted, "Did the engines quit? Are we going to crash?"

Why didn't I pay more attention to the exit strategies explained at the beginning of every freaking flight? I was on full alert status. Why did everyone take this catastrophe so calmly? We needed to prepare the cabin. Where did they keep those life jackets?

"Miss, Miss, sit down." The stewardess rushed toward me, assuring me. "We are still waiting for take-off."

When I arrived in Dallas, I was notified my luggage hadn't been transferred from the smoky plane onto the new flight. Good thing I personally carried my fishing tackle box. At the beginning of my career, a plastic case with all those little storage compartments made for fishing lures was my primitive, albeit trusty, makeup kit. When I handed it over to the driver, I noticed the brand name printed on the top of my blue box: "Plano." Funny. My Plano box is with me in Plano, Texas. I was relieved I had my film camera with me—the essentials were not in my lost luggage. However, I was worried about the special dress I had packed. The pageant organizers told me to dress up. I would be walking on stage to do touch-ups, and if a camera caught a glimpse of me I needed to be out of the usual uniform I wore, which consisted of comfy clothes plus a hat. I'd had a seamstress whip up a little sleeveless cocktail dress. We're talking sequins and feathers, the whole nine yards. I was going to be styling. I couldn't wait to get a picture with the contestants in that little number.

Backstage, there was a tornado of activity. Personalities were flying as high as the stylists teased the hair. This was Texas, where the bigger the hair, the closer to God. Lips were also getting brighter, while the chatter buzzed.

While I set up for Avery, the contestant from Washington, my heart raced. I felt lucky to be in the right city. I overheard one East Coast contestant whispering, "I agree, I think Washington is the front runner," said the champion of the biggest hair I had ever seen.

"Sasha, you're right up there," her friend offered.

Avery sat in my chair as if on cue and I quickly, but calmly, got her ready for the curtain call. I let out a big sigh as I finished Avery's makeup just as the stage manager was rounding up the contestants for the parade of states. "Alabama, Alaska, Arizona, Arkansas, you're on."

"Where are my shoes?" Avery revealed an empty box. There was no wardrobe department for this event. Each woman was in charge of her own garb.

"Line up, California, Colorado, Connecticut..."

"...Kansas, Kentucky..."

"We have time to figure something out." I kept my composure as Avery panicked and I was doing state alphabet math in my head, from the letter K to W, to determine just how much time we had before Washington.

"...Mississippi, Missouri..."

We turned her wardrobe chest upside down. No shoes.

"New York, hurry up," barked the stage manager.

I peeked under her gown. "Avery, wear the shoes you have on."

"No, my dress was hemmed perfectly for the Diors!"

"North Dakota, where are you?" repeated the stage manager.

"Go barefoot and make a statement," I pleaded.

"Oklahoma, Oregon, you ladies are up next."

"No, Trista, see: my dress is dragging."

"...Tennessee...right now!" called the stage manager.

Avery tried on the shoes she'd worn with her interview suit. "All business."

"But an option, right?" I asked.

"Pennsylvania..."

"Shall we just borrow these ones?" I saw some abandoned shoes off to the side of a mirrored closet.

"Ooh, too big! I will slip right out of them." Avery had hoped for glass slippers and a Cinderella ending.

"Let's use wardrobe tape and stick your feet onto them," I suggested.

"Are you kidding? I'm being judged on poise."

I needed to put on my Dick Tracy hat. What if someone borrowed her Dior shoes? Or maybe hid them? Hmm...could it possibly be those two whisperers I'd heard earlier predicting Washington to be the winner? Perhaps they were trying to sabotage Avery? A light bulb clicked on. I found their staging area and tossed and turned their clothing world upside down. Bingo...I felt like I had recovered Dorothy's ruby slippers.

"Utah, Vermont, Virginia...I'm looking for Washington," the stage manager said as Avery elegantly glided on stage.

I took pictures of her from the balcony, and tried to memorialize her once-in-a-lifetime experience from all different phases of the event and again after my luggage finally arrived.

One of the contestants had alopecia, the disease causing hair loss. I helped her with false lashes and applied makeup for her eyebrows. During the interview on stage, she took off her wig, which was completely unplanned and shocked the crowd. I snapped a shot of us and considered the photo priceless. Plus, it gave me the opportunity to rock my sequins and feathers.

The pageant was an exhausting experience and I don't remember my head ever hitting the pillow, but I woke up in the dark, drenched in sweat. Where am I? Am I on another plane with more smoke issues? I rolled over and groggily dialed zero, to reach the hotel operator. "I'm so hot, I can't breathe, and it's sweltering in here," I mumbled.

"Okay, help is on the way," said the operator.

I fell back to sleep while waiting for the front desk to come up and fix the heater. I heard a pounding on the door. I stumbled out of bed to answer the door, but I didn't see anyone, only a hallway. Where is the help—at the wrong room?

"Open up! Fire department!"

As I came out of my stupor I realized I was not in the Plano hotel. I opened the front door to my own house. "We got a call your house is on fire," the firemen reported.

With a lost sense of my whereabouts, and even worse, the discovery that there had been no film in my camera to document my memories, I surmised pageants must be hazardous to my health. If that weren't enough, I had totally lost my acute visual detective skills. No more pageants and crime solving for me.

# Race Relations Officer

As I anxiously waited for Shamus to enter my makeup trailer, I reorganized and pulled any products or colors I could potentially possibly need. I never want to be asked and not have anything requested. Carefully and artfully I displayed all his makeup in front of the mirror, where he'd be sitting at my station. I waited and waited...looked at the time and studied again the call sheet for his expected arrival. Geez, it was only 30 minutes 'til he was due on set, and it always takes longer to apply character makeup during my first session.

The door flung open and my director assistant, Jared, flew in. "Shamus doesn't want to come to your trailer, Trista." Jared is kind and professional. He orchestrates the basecamp dance of shuffling actors between hotels, trailers, and set better than anyone in the business. "Shamus has summoned you to his personal trailer." We both chuckle...only "A-listers" get me to work in their trailer. Ridiculous. I guess I didn't get the memo. Is he considered A-list?

Jessica Biel and Vera Farmiga both came to the makeup trailer. I definitely would rate them an A. A++++. Both Jess and Vera were the sweetest, most genuine actresses with whom I've ever had the privilege of working.

Christian Slater refused to come to the trailer, but I adored him anyway. He was such a kind spirit. I would go out of my way for Christian anytime, so you just never know.

I tossed everything into a bag as Jared sympathetically hurried me out of my trailer. We approached Shamus' massive, sleek RV, a stark contrast from my white tin box. Jared knocked and asked permission to enter. I shout out the customary movie lingo, "Stepping," which indicates you're entering into a crew or cast space. I introduced myself pleasantly, while extending my hand for him to shake. Jared left promptly and moved on to his next actor to drag into place.

Shamus did not reach for my hand. He roared, "You're not black!"

I glanced at my hand and indeed, it's not black. "Yes, that would be correct...sir."

"I want a black makeup artist," he demanded.

"Um...well, that would be a producer decision, not mine...sir."

"Don't you have any black makeup artists in your department?"

"I don't. Your call time is in a few minutes. Can I get you camera-ready and we can continue this conversation with a producer?"

"How do you know how to do my makeup? Any experience with black skin?" He was rudely dismissive.

I started to unhinge. "Yes...definitely...Natalie Cole." Come on, Trista, list the black men. "Curtis, 50 Cent." Damn, I should have said "fitty." I referred to him as "5 Cents" before my daughter Taci corrected me. "Cuba Gooding Jr., sir." I felt I had scored points with Cuba. He's an Academy Award winning actor for God's sake. That should suffice. I rambled, unconfidently. I wished I were prepared for this line of questioning. I have a résumé of famous black male clients. He was clearly challenging my credibility, and with that revelation I whipped out a towel and was glad it happened to be black. I started placing my colors out for him to see that I truly am a prepared, competent artist. But am I? My very first memory of my life was with my younger sisters, ages two and one. They were both in diapers on the floor and I was on a bare mattress in our bedroom. I felt like I was in charge with no skills. I was three.

I motioned for Shamus to sit...he wouldn't. Okay, yep, I can stand on my very tippy toes and reach his head while he stood what seemed to be a looming 10 feet tall. I held a blue MAC strip. "Can I prepare your skin?" No comment from him. I'm imagining he would say something like, "Nothing you have here will work for me," and I could call it a day.

I wished with all my might that Shamus would demand some product he absolutely wouldn't be caught dead without, and the producers would urgently arrange to have it shipped, but we learn it's not available in the great U.S. of A. And it's fittingly going to be from some country in Africa, like Namibia. And we will book a special airline seat for this vastly important, who-cares-what-this-will-cost-stop-the-show makeup. Or better yet, here's an idea: let's order up a beautiful, talented, black makeup artist who can share a seat on the FedEx jet with the precious product—special delivery, overnight.

Sigh...I snap back to reality.

"Do you have any sensitivities, Shamus, I should be aware of?" (Besides white people?) No words from him...just an unsettling negative vibe coming from one source. I want to go home. *I want my blankie.* I trembled...oh, hands stay still...stand up straight...don't cry. Oh, God, that would be the worst. He mumbled and I gingerly approached to touch his skin. I felt like a horse trainer going in for a first-time attempt to tame a bucking bronco. I pressed a blue strip onto his forehead to remove the shine...and then another and another and another. He had limitless oil flowing from his pores. I'm going to need a case of these bad boys for this project. I lightly applied Bobbi Brown cream foundation, Espresso No.10, the very darkest shade possible, and it was a perfect match to even out the darkness—on his face, not his heart. My stomach hurt. I feathered in some black hair strokes to fill in the brows. I used a stipple sponge, which is porous and black, with a black gel to even out his beard stubble. I found the need to pepper my thoughts with the names of black products in any form to make me feel less white. I finished with Bobbi Brown loose powder...gosh, I love this powder. It's the only one containing no mica, and it works phenomenally on black skin and in high-definition camera lighting. His color was basic brown mixed with a skosh of dark Ben Nye.

I asked Shamus my standard question about how he'd like me to handle last looks on set, but surprise, he's still mum. He displayed unwavering emotion. Pretty sure I will be drinking my dinner. "Would you like anything on your lips?" Oh, gee, again... no response. Most male actors are very particular on lip balms. I wanted to be dialed in and use the correct option, but, hey, I will just guess. I'm finished. Get me out of here. A wave of nausea washed over me.

I presented the hand mirror for him to check my work. I was in a cold sweat and became physically ill. I pleaded with my body. Hold on. I willed it steady 'til the RV door opened. If he chose to kick me out after he saw his reflection...great...the fastest exit out, the better.

He performed a rotational turn of his head from side to side and his reflection revealed a solemn study of his face. Then, with no discouraging remarks, I began to feel a slight bit of relief. Slight. I was free to pack up my wares and skedaddle the hell out of this forsaken hole. As I reached for my mirror to tuck into my packed bags, he forcefully threw my hands back toward me and boomed, "Don't you ever expect us to be friends."

I was a beaten-down puppy sent away to lick my wounds. I was unable to speak. I was holding back a pent-up dam of emotions. I vowed to hold it together, and I did with every step until I reached my trailer and my door closed behind me. The dam broke...no, it gushed uncontrollably, cracked wide open in a flood of immeasurable sobs.

Day two, and I managed a pep talk with my beautiful BFF makeup artist, Amy. We concocted a game plan. I will not be defeated. Red rover, red rover, we call Amy right over. Everyone, and I mean everyone, chooses Amy to be on his or her team. I have clients requesting only Amy. She has this comforting, unassuming persona exuding radiant light. My situation with Shamus just got solved. He talked to the producers and knew hiring a black makeup artist wasn't an option. Next best choice was Amy. He'll surely adore her.

Jared prompted us to head over to Shamus for makeup in his trailer. I figured on strength in numbers. Amy will assist me, making her undeniably necessary. Then in a few days, I will pass the baton over to my angelic girl and I will skip to my lou, oh, happy days would be here again.

I'm sure I heard Shamus growling as we entered. He pointed at Amy as if she were an alien being. "What's going on? What's this?"

"Good morning, sir, this is Amy and she will be helping me on set today." Oh, no. This wasn't feeling good...I'm getting nauseated.

"Oh, hell, no. *Get out. Get out*," he stormed.

He didn't even allow Amy to shine a small dose of her goodliness. We're struck down, cold. Now it's Amy who was representing the distraught puppy as she left, and I was alone, again. Take two of enduring a slow torture. I felt the need for liquid courage.

And the torture continued. Take 20, day 20, Groundhog Day all over again. It never got easier. He never changed. His words and actions were haunting.

Eventually I changed his makeup and last look routine to a wet towel only. I handed it to him on set and he wiped away the oil river. It was over. And just between us...I was still waiting for a beautiful black makeup artist to show up.

# Secret Keeper

I have a ritual of tasks I complete prior to starting principal photography. The pre-production preparation phase starts way before filming; details upon details before we set foot on the set. I read the script...nap...read more script...yawn...familiarize myself with the character development...another nap...break down the scenes in an Excel spreadsheet...yell at my computer...arrange a timeline...do breathing exercises while lying flat on the floor...set up character continuity files...remind myself I'm an artist, not a techno geek. I'll peruse the actors' past film projects on Internet Media Database, also referred to as IMDb. It tracks movie credits like a standard résumé. I find entertaining tidbits in their past performances to segue into my introduction.

I was preparing to call Bobby Lee. His main characters were

leading villains and he was notorious for playing "Zabe" in a mega cult favorite movie. "Zabe" was beyond iconic. He raped and tortured and was the definition of *pure* evil. After I gathered my wits and my heart started a normal rhythm, I gave Zabe—I mean Bobby—a shout via phone to discuss his product preferences. Did he have skin sensitivities? What were his makeup concerns? Did he believe in type casting? No, Trista, skip the last question. Let's not wake up "Zabe!" His voice seemed normal. Can you judge a voice? What's normal? Stop sweating, Trista.

My next conversation was in the makeup trailer when we physically met. I had his kit set up with all his requests, along with several options pertaining to any of his needs. One of his concerns was his bald spot on the back of his head. This is an issue I address often. I always laugh because I instantly think about the late-night infomercial with the demonstration of the wet black spray coming from a small aerosol can. Have you seen it? It was not to be used for graffiti or sidewalk art, but only on your head. Bobby would be working with co-actor Angela Shann in the water. He didn't want any makeup to wash off during a scene...or his painted-on hair. No bother with an alcohol-based waterproof color and it doesn't come in a spray can.

There were five stations in this makeup trailer, each with a hydraulic chair in front of the mirrored space. You know, the chairs you pump to go up or down. They weigh a ton. When I want one moved, I have my transportation guys do it.

My typical practice was in place. Products requested, yes. Products not requested, but he might possibly need based on my breakdown of his character...check. Bobby walked into my empty trailer. The rest of the makeup and hair crew were on set with the cast, filming.

I swung my chair toward him. "Hi, Bobby, come on in, I'm Trista. We talked on the phone last week." I motioned for him to sit and he moved toward me. He slammed down hard onto the floor between my station and the next, missing my chair completely. That's clearly got to hurt.

He jumped up and screamed, "Fuck you, Trista. Why did you move my chair? You just tried to kill me! Fuck! What's wrong with you?"

Well, that was a smooth way to greet my actor for the first time. Sure, I can lift and place a 200-pound chair in the four seconds and six steps it took him to enter the trailer and saunter my way. That's exactly how I pictured my first impression. Torture my actor without tweezing, or just end it by killing him. Bobby ran around ranting while scratching his itchy arms. Huh? Arms? Not rubbing his heinie that just took a beating?

Have any of my past circumstances prepared me for this complex state of affairs? Help me. I need air. There was no diffusing. I couldn't scoot out the trailer door fast enough.

Sigh.

Okay.

Better.

Let me think.

Several years prior, I'd worked with David Keith. He was the famous dude in *An Officer and a Gentleman*. His character swallowed his fiancée's engagement ring, and then hung himself in the bathtub. Remember him? After he played that role I was his artist for a small Christian family film. Maybe he was trying to save his soul? After we wrapped on the very first day he insisted I get in his convertible so he could drive me back to base camp. "No, thanks, David, I prefer to walk."

He was driving beside me and taunting, *"Get in...get in the damn car, Trista...so help me...get in."* His barking was relentless and it reminded me of my childhood. I was conditioned to be polite and nonchalant through hellish moments. I walked back to base camp. He sped off, burning rubber like a crazed teenager. He called later that night and insisted I color and cut his hair.

"I will pad enough time to get it done tomorrow morning before your call time, David," I said encouragingly.

"No. *Now.* At my hotel," he stormed.

I didn't want to be alone in his hotel room, but the word "no" was a foreign concept. I was lucky I brought my hair assistant. She propped the door ajar leading to the hallway. It felt awkward; she felt it was necessary. She must have had a normal childhood. During the course of filming I pegged Keith's issues and I got through it.

As a secret keeper, how do I handle Bobby Lee? He doesn't appear to be drunk. Tyrant? It's still to be determined.

During the next few weeks of the show I asked Bobby questions to fill in the many blanks I had in regard to his grand entrance. I wanted to know his story. I was curious. I was hoping for answers. No, I was on a freaking mission. Spill your secrets! "Bobby, how did you get in the business? Have any pets? Siblings?" Ever been institutionalized?

Eventually he relaxed, opened up, and began to trust me. Bobby confessed. He was an addict. Heroin. That explained his incessant itching. But did he have concerns about doing his own driving stunts? "Ya know, Bobby, speeding through downtown...women and children...for God's sake?"

He laughed. "No, I'm not using now, Trista." Wow. He'd just admitted his addiction, and I knew full well he was still using. Like I said, he was always itchy. Should I announce his confided habit to the powers that be so they can find a stunt double?

Bobby wasn't the only actor harboring a secret. Angela told me she was pregnant, but hush, for no one is to know. "I don't want to use a body double in my water scenes," she stated calmly.

Okay, well let's shoot those quickly, because you're going to grow out of your swimsuit, dearie. Not even the wardrobe department knew. Slowly during our shooting schedule she was subtly growing in sizes, but it could be from too much of the goodies provided by the craft services, right?

Bradley was another interesting dude, and of course had his own secrets worn on his face. He must have the worst plastic surgery results in movie star history, and to make his appearance worse, he insisted on pink foundation. Pink. Kaia, his makeup artist, is the best in the business, but you can't fix wrong.

As Bradley waited on set to do his scene with Angela, there was a slight problem. She was MIA. Angela wasn't in her trailer nor at craft services gaining unexplained weight. No, that's because she was in the bushes...throwing up.

Bradley whispered, "What's that funny noise?"

"I don't know Brad...umm...I don't hear anything."

I had an assortment of epics on this movie. For the first time, I worked with a heroin addict, a closet preggers, and, with two weeks remaining on the project, I was dismissed. Pretty sure it's a pleasant word for "fired." I will surely keep this a secret. I was told it was budget constraints—another nice word for "We ran out of money!" I didn't see it coming, perhaps because I was fairly new in this business. It was 2006 and I had less than a dozen features on IMDb.

My last hurrah as a secret keeper was meeting with my makeup department head to review my detailed presentation of continuity notes and secrets. Bobby Lee: create the waterproof illusion of hair, with the door open, and ignore itchiness. Angela: steer clear of girly discussions on weight. Bradley: do not stare at his face.

As I exited and said my "woe is me" sad farewells, I had a surprise guest stop me in my tracks. It was the same producer who had fired me—I mean became broke.

Bobby had forcefully stated a non-compromising threat to all the producers on this project. "If Trista goes, I go!" Bobby insisted.

Bobby stayed.

And so did I. Disasters were averted on my mission as a secret keeper, and I didn't have to keep another secret.

# Personal Assistant

I had the role as a personal assistant in several of my gigs. This is apparently a big part of being a makeup artist.

*The Ward* was filmed in Medical Lake, Washington, at a mental hospital: a brick, dungeon-like campus built in the late 1800s. It was very well suited as a backdrop for a psychiatric thriller set in 1966. The director of this project was the king of shock, Academy Award winner James Carpenter. He directed such horror sci-fi classics as *Halloween, Escape from LA*, and *They Live*. I was the head of this makeup department with a large cast and numerous makeup artists supporting me.

I'm always a little fearful to have the first conversation with the man who has a vision for the project—in this case, James Carpenter. I had a few weeks to wrap my head around the script; however,

Mr. Carpenter had been completely submerged in it for years. It's a fine balance between having my own ideas as an artist and incorporating the vision of the director. On top of that I should be making the actors feel comfortable in their ideas as well. I truly am placed in the middle.

This was my first day on a new job. I had done initial preparation to have answers to questions. I wanted to appear polished and confident, and for them to feel they had hired the right person. I arrived at the production office and envisioned myself looking James Carpenter square in his eyes while I firmly shook his hand. I wanted to emit a positive vibe, to show I was open to any of his suggestions and to represent my department as team players, but as I entered to engage in my first conversation with John Carpenter, he didn't shake my hand. I wasn't even sure he knew my name or even wanted to know it. He was stern and gruff. The smoke from his burning cigarette overtook the room. He made no attempt to redirect the smoke blowing in my face as he coughed out, "I want the no-makeup look." Meeting over.

Why couldn't he be more like Henry Winkler (well known as "The Fonz")? On my first day filming for *Hollywood Squares* he greeted me with fresh flowers and a big smile. He was the producer and Tom Bergeron (*Dancing with the Stars*) was the host.

Carpenter held scripted rehearsals with the six leading starlets and while he was with them, he relayed his insistence they all look completely au naturel during filming. It made sense. The story takes place in a looney bin and those ladies were patients. I'm on board with that.

A makeup and hair camera test was scheduled and my results would be rolled onto the big screen in an AMC Theater so we could see every skin pore of my cast and critique their look.

My lead actress was Amber Heard, an intelligent, attractive blonde, a ridiculously riveting gal, who was accompanied by her significant other, a photographer who had black hair, dark eyes, and was always dressed in black. Also in tow were her cute Yorkshire terriers, Pistol and Boo. Amber needed her pets for emotional support, so she registered them as service dogs and they were granted a free pass to travel. That was my first intro to pets having a job label. She had just finished her work filming on *The Rum Diary* with Johnny Depp.

Learning of her working relationship with Depp took me back in time to the very first movie set I ever visited. I was trying to get into the movie business. I had done a little television work and wanted to get my feet wet on the big screen. An opportunity presented itself to meet the head makeup artist Patty York, so I applied as an intern on *Benny and Joon,* an adorable movie Depp filmed at the beginning of his mega rise to iconic stardom.

On *Benny and Joon,* I felt like I had entered a foreign galaxy, by engraved invitation only: the mystique of a new territory; a merry mixture of wonderment and the unknown; and the brief meet of a childlike man, sitting on a tricycle, with a quick charismatic nod at me. The Johnny Depp. Yes, I wanted to be a part of this, and no, Trista, you don't get the golden ticket to be a makeup intern. But I was granted the small token of permission to hang out a bit while they were filming. And after the wrap parties and goodbyes I re-entered the ordinary world.

Now, that seems like a lifetime ago. Well, it was. With time, persistence, and experience, I was the proud owner of a makeup department with an award winning director who wanted me to not put any makeup on his ingénues.

Here we go...camera test was in place. Six actresses in the trailer with naked faces, ready for my team to apply makeup without it looking like we were applying makeup. Airbrush or a very light-handed, well-blended liquid makeup, and using the correct powder work well for high-definition. One of my little darling actresses was not hip with the plan. She insisted we use her own personal daytime mineral powder. Most powders, and especially minerals, are designed to be luminescent, which is great for a fresh daytime look...but horrible for filming. "I have sensitive skin and I will die with anything else," was her pleading cry for mercy. I can wish and talk and demonstrate my way to her trust, but sometimes I just can't win.

Predictably, she was the only one John called out during the makeup review at the AMC Theater. "Why the hell is she so shiny?" John blustered with disgust.

I fidgeted, but now I had the ammunition I needed to do it my way. It's painful to be in the middle.

Amber's camera test went well, even though I was worried about her wearing false lashes. How is that natural? Heard insisted and we pulled it off. All the makeup working for the camera test was placed in her labeled kit, along with brushes. Pictures and notes were filed into her book along with the character breakdown for continuity.

Day one, I got pulled into a meeting with the producer.

"Amber would prefer you use Touché Éclat instead of Laura Mercier concealer." I was confused. For the love...she didn't mention it in our tests. I'm a nice person, can't she talk to me directly?

Day two, surprise: a meeting with the producer. "Amber thinks she is allergic to your makeup and it's giving her blemishes." Oh, sure, this was her very first skin issue and it's my fault. Definitely. I always wonder if the actors' "allergic reactions" are from partying all night, drinking excessively, not getting proper rest, not hydrating enough, or simply from eating too much craft service? Or maybe— and I know this is a stretch of the imagination, but stay with me here—could it be possible she just has acne? I called in a derma-tologist, and not just any dermatologist, but Pam Schell, recog-nized nationally as a skincare expert, nurse practitioner, and one who holds a doctorate in health psychology. Who better to help me whip this Hollywood actress into mental alignment...excuse me, skin shape? Pam dropped everything and came to my trailer. She injected steroids directly into the raised cyst to reduce the swelling. This treatment worked in minutes and Amber was camera-ready. I put Pam on speed dial for the remainder of my career.

Day three: back problems. Once I called Pam, the skin care expert, the producer must have taken it as a cue for me to be Amber's personal assistant. I placed a call to the best deep-tissue massage therapist around. Not just any therapist, but one who was trustworthy and wouldn't divulge confidential information about Amber Heard and one who would travel to her hotel suite. Amber didn't want to visit an office. Also, I won't be able to give a specific time so this therapist also needs to be flexible—not just a little flexible, but on hold—because she might wrap in two hours or 14 hours. Cassie Baker fit the bill of the Pinterest-perfect massage therapist.

As a career makeup artist/work wife/personal assistant I have ordered food from special restaurants to be delivered to hotel rooms, I have arranged phone calls, picked up dry cleaning, bought groceries, ordered drug store prescriptions, babysat children, washed cars, delivered barista coffee, and made appointments, to name just a few tasks. I remember being asked to purchase a toothbrush. I grabbed one with a red handle. I was immediately sent to exchange it for a blue one. Does color really make a difference? I suppose. I once hired a painter for a celebrity who needed their hotel room painted a different color before they arrived. So, arranging a massage therapist for Amber is quite tame and I really was happy to do it. Seemingly I did it as a friend...a paid one.

Amber's talent in the film was unbelievably instinctive. I really enjoyed watching her performances while I studied her face for any changes I needed to address.

Her significant other, the photographer who always wore black, showed up in the trailer often and was seen on set behind the monitor and they shared breaks together. They were inseparable.

Our last place to work was in Seattle, a quick plane ride from the mental hospital location where all the interiors had been shot. It's not practical to film in chronological order, and the first scene of the movie was our last scheduled to shoot. It was an exterior piece representing the entrance of the mental hospital when "Kristen"/ Amber is brought by ambulance and it marks her first appearance in the movie. Carpenter liked the outside of the building in Seattle better than at Eastern State Mental Hospital where we shot 99 percent of the movie. This set was a relief from the claustrophobic smoky sets at the mental hospital. Mr. Carpenter's never-ending cigarette stayed lit until the wrap of the movie. I felt like I was coming down with cancer.

As we settled into our new location, I was called to a meeting with the producer...joy! It never happens. Wait, let me guess, as Amber's personal assistant I need to fly in Pam the dermatologist, Cassie the massage therapist, and purchase dog food? No, instead it was a tiny new demand. I was asked to put makeup on a new Amber. "Just make the stand-in replacement look exactly like Amber's character 'Kristen,' please?" As a personal assistant, this was an acrimonious request.

Amber had been detained because of an incident at the Seattle airport. It was a domestic violence situation with her *female* photographer significant other—#Didn'tSeeThatComing. Did you?

This story comes full circle. The first movie set I visited was *Benny and Joon,* with Johnny Depp, and I end this story on one with Amber Heard who is now his "waswife," who was formerly a "waslesbian." You can't make this stuff up, and as a personal assistant, I thought I had seen everything.

Several years later, I remember being in a situation where I needed my own personal assistant. The filming location was in Glacier National Park in Montana. I perused the call sheet for pertinent information. There was a list of crew members and the name I flagged was the locations manager's. I added his contact information to my phone, because I plan on getting lost wherever I go. The client was Phillip Morris USA and the agency was Leo Burnett USA out of Chicago, the Marlboro cigarette people. Our agenda wasn't to shoot the Marlboro cowboy dude on the horse riding into the sunset smoking a cigarette. No, those days are gone forever. But this was, "We have done so much harm in the world destroying lives, polluting our environment, and littering the Earth so we're doing a 'Give Back' campaign." If they had convinced director John Carpenter to quit smoking I think they could've called it good. That's a wrap.

The call sheet recorded the weather. High of 35 degrees with a low of 18 degrees. Pack the parka and boots, not the t-shirt and sandals. I reviewed the talent list and I saw 12 names, arriving at the same time. It stated the closest medical facility, North Valley Hospital, was in Whitefish, Montana, just in case any of us fall off the glacier. Oh, and the biggest bullet point on the call sheet was in big red letters highlighted in yellow: "Watch out for bears. They're *not* your friends." With 32 crew members, five clients, six outfitters, six agency peeps, and 12 talents surrounding me, I considered safety in numbers.

I began my journey at the car wash to vacuum out the last month's lunch remnants. The sun had yet to rise and my allergies were in full force. Well, I only have one. I'm allergic to morning. If I had a personal assistant, this task would surely be on her list. I pulled into the first of 10 vacuum stations. While I was rushing, the handle fell off the vacuum. Instead of moving to another vacuum I used it without the hose tip. There's a reason the vacuums have slim slits to filter debris. The wide-mouthed hose got too close to my keys sitting on the console and sucked them into never-never land. This was a slightly better situation than when I lost my keys in the middle of the back woods. It happened. There was no car wash attendant around, so I called for a ride from a friend to take me home and fetch my spare car key. I wish I could've inconvenienced a paid personal assistant.

The entire Marlboro video was shot outside in the glorious elements of Mother Nature. The wind was biting. Each and every time I did a touch-up I had to expose my fingers. It's impossible to apply makeup with gloves on, and even though I wore Columbia boots, my toes were numb and I was miserable. One of the talents came up from behind me and tugged on my ponytail. I giggled because I needed to be nice. Later I was leaning on my rig waiting to do touch-ups and he brushed up against me. "Are you cold?"

"Nope, I'm never cold." I can act too.

I went into town after my first day wrapped and bought wool socks, along with hand warmers and Under Armour garments, lots of them. I think it was a task for my personal assistant. Oh, wait. I don't have one. I wished I could've purchased armor to protect me from pests.

On the second day, I chose not to be a passenger in the travel van with the other crew, actors, and a pest, so I could use the back of my rig as a makeup staging area. There were foggy, blizzard-like conditions with black ice as I drove myself to the national park from our lodge in Whitefish. I got separated from the crew caravan, so I called the locations manager, but there was no cell reception. How hard could it be to find the crew? I was driving to the top of a mountain for God's sake; isn't this when common sense kicks in? No, if I were smart I would have a personal assistant driving. I followed the road signs, which led me to the main picnic area of the national park, and got lucky. Whew.

The day was spent clearing and building new hiking pathways, and in between set-ups I was able to crank the heat up in my locked rig. It didn't seem to help. Why isn't there a heat setting called Tropical Temperature Near the Equator? Every time I saw the pest I pretended to be busy and when it was his turn for makeup, I told the next to standby so I was never alone.

On a company move to another location, I drove my beast of a rig across the river, not on a bridge, but over a treacherous narrow, faded plank. I was petrified. Perhaps I would be remembered with a small headline on the back page of my local newspaper. My personal assistant could write, "Makeup artist dies in a car while falling two feet." Hopefully she adds some validity by explaining it was the frigid waters that got me.

With my death thoughts looming, I received a request to film additional scenes for a movie I had previously wrapped. They needed the scenes done pronto to help with the editing, and this was the only window of time to fit with the schedules of the actors and crew. The only way it was going to work was if I slept a few hours after finishing the Marlboro production, then drove all night to arrive for call time back in Spokane.

Shortly into my trek back, I struggled to keep my eyes open. Usually distractions are my demise while driving. Squirrel. Perhaps being in the cold and spending all my energy dodging the pest contributed to my tiredness. Thinking of pests, a bug splat on my windshield and I thought it was my eyeballs popping, so I pulled over to rest.

This happened before in a similar circumstance, when I drove from Los Angeles to Spokane for a show. Back then, as now, I had a rig full of supplies and flying wasn't an option. Coffee wasn't enough to keep me going so I continually stopped and ran around my car for energy. I was on mile 900 from LA, and had only four hours to go but I physically succumbed and pulled into a rest stop. It was dark and countless long-haul truckers were parked there for the evening. For whatever reason, and likely due to my impressive state of exhaustion, and after seeing a few too many sketchy people, I became overwhelmed with fear and had visions of every tragic ending to the worst imaginable horror film. I reached into my back seat and pulled every item of clothing I could find over my head before dozing. I thought if someone shot me, at least I wouldn't see it coming.

Driving back from Montana I didn't see any rest stops. I don't even know if they have airports. If I had a personal assistant I would have her drive, or my bestie Amy. She appointed herself as our driver while filming the music video for "Downtown" with Macklemore and Ryan Lewis. I drove the wrong way on a one-way, and with that last thought, I pulled over into a parking lot. After my nap I didn't feel any more capable to continue driving. I definitely was knocking on heaven's door, so I called my dot, Taci, to come get me.

After finishing those two projects I physically and emotionally collapsed into my personal nest. A friend, who was concerned with my well-being, peered into my room as I slept and swears he saw the shadow of a woman-shaped figure disconcertingly looming over me. The hair on his arms stood up as he described this ghostly vision he truly believed to be my "guardian angel." Oh, I'm sure it was my much-needed personal assistant reporting for duty.

# BUILDER

In many situations, I'm expected to improvise and create with no warning and with complete chaos all around me, like building a house in a hurricane.

I was assigned to be Darcy Black's artist on a small independent film. Assigned. Yes, this one was like school, complete with dreadful homework. Looking back, Darcy was an assignment.

We were filming a romantic comedy exploring the adult film industry through the eyes of an idealistic award winning film graduate. Not sure if "idealistic" and "film graduate" should be in the same sentence but...Darcy played two separate characters, each one with a different identity and name. "Jane," one of her casted roles, is a shy, pretty, unassuming actress—again, "unassuming" and "actress" so close together in a short sentence? But her second character, "Yvette," portrayed a sexy, seducing starlet. Now. There. *Those* words mesh. It was important to the plot of the story for her porn identity not to be revealed until the end of the movie. Oh goodie, I like crafting a disguise.

In an earlier film I built disguises for a spy family. I made the conservative Christian family of four into a punk rock band with tattoos, metal chains, and wild hair. During pre-production I asked the director if he wanted me to provide sample drawings for his approval. He shooed me away, but I was ready for his accolades during my big reveal on the first scene of the first shooting day.

"Who the hell came up with these disguises?" The director boomed. My tribe (the crew) backed slightly away and an invisible laser spotlight focused on me. It felt like when I was seven years old and I made my father a sandwich. I was so proud. I held my breath waiting for his first bite and the kudos to soon follow. My father squished the sandwich into pieces and started throwing it at me, just like the director threw my work back into my face.

So, when I was asked to make a disguise for Darcy in this romantic comedy, I had a post-traumatic-non-approval-disorder, but I was determined not to fail. I had a vision to make this incognito sexy look with a short black bob wig *Chicago*/Catherine Zeta-Jones style. I remodeled her famous eyebrows by using mortician's wax to hide her bold Darcy brows and created a pencil-thin dark frame. Full blood-red lips—does that translate to sex or death? I transformed her recognizable baby blue eyes to black, and finished with falsies as long as this filming seemed to take.

Sometimes pre-production is appropriately timed to organize all the details. This particular pre-pro was gas-foot-to-the-floor, Mach 4, hair-on-fire, get the hell out of my way pre-pro.

I made an appointment with Darcy's eye doc for measurements to fit her black contacts properly. Builders need exact measurements to be successful. Black's personal assistant Sho made the arrangement, but it came and went with no Darcy. No explanations. No excuses. Just Darcy's way of saying, "It doesn't matter people are waiting for me, scheduling their day to accommodate me, need to get their contracted jobs done...no, it doesn't matter." Time was slipping so I got an ophthalmologist to come meet us on location, but again, a no-go. She got confused. Yikes, I give up. Blue eyes, not black: check.

The female director, Jackie, asked if I could get rid of Darcy's facial mustache. They saw those little wispy hairs above her lovely top lip in a photo and didn't want to ever see them again, and you are definitely going to see them on HiDef. (You see everything on HiDef. I think this is part of what makes some actresses insane. There are thousands of things making actresses insane.) *Yowza,* these types of conversations are never easy to approach. Yes, you are perfect. We cast you. Now, let's see...can we change you? And she and I had yet to properly bond. Our only experience thus far was my requesting measured eyeballs, and she failed to comply. Now, let me delicately ask, "Please let me derma-plane your face. Trust me...I do it all the time to my daughters! Exactly how do I perform this task, you ask? Oh, with a sharp, medical-grade scalpel. Yes, trust me, as a builder I use sharp tools. I will give you at least five minutes on your first visit to my makeup trailer to get to know me."

The mustache stayed.

One very late night, days into our shooting schedule, Jackie the director asked if I could speed up the process of applying the disguise. The inexperienced director was always in a rush, just like homeowners, and even at the expense of quality. Quality: that's a stretch. This budget was low. In one of the last scenes we filmed, we shot our lead actor in the dark. Yep, not as in night, but as in before the lighting crew could light him.

As I prepared to do Darcy's makeup I was asked, "How much time will this take?" My entire department cringes when I get asked "How much longer? Can you hurry?" Building contractors are to be on schedule, but are they ever? It's never understood, the process we building artists go through. It's always a crapshoot. How the hell do I know how long it's going to take before the star is confident enough to be in front of the camera for the whole world to criticize and to gawk at their every move and eyelash? "You look simply *mahhh-velous* darling...now run along, go ahead, I will do final touches on set, yes, sweetheart, you look great, they are ready for you, yes, I'm right behind you, I got you covered, yes...We can come back to the trailer before your close-up...go ahead now, you're gorgeous." But what I'm thinking is, *Get the fuck out of my chair...you're a constant endless mess of insecurities and a bottomless pit of needs. You are sucking every fiber out of my being. There isn't one more freaking thing I can do!*

The directors want all the time the actor can give in front of the camera. The producers bark, "Time is money" and want them in and out of the makeup chair, well, for that matter, in and out of their life, like, yesterday. On the flip side, the talent wants to feel confident and won't leave the trailer until they're damn ready. So..."How much longer, Trista?" I reply whatever it is they want to hear, just like when a homeowner is asking the contractor when he can move in. "Fifteen minutes."

After this particular request of "Please hurry the eff up," Darcy decided she was tired. Her answer to the director's request was for me to apply her porn makeup and wig while she slept. Okay, for reals? Do I need to explain the concept of gravity? While I'm lying down and holding up a mirror, why yes, I have demonstrated this concept on myself: I have an instant facelift, confident breasts, and a bikini body. When I sit up, it all goes away. Oh and let's see...it's not going to be just my invested time, let's snag two other assistants to help me 'cause, ya know, we have no other actors to get ready, it's just all about *you*. I need one stylist to lift your head and another to fit all your hair into a cap while yet another assistant slides on the wig... umm yeah, this is going to be a real time-saver.

Following her power nap—power because she took all mine—Darcy wanted soup. She asked that I not touch her while she sipped, while she and her personal assistant, Sho, both *sipped*. My "15 minutes" is now 120. Sweet Jesus, help me, when the next knock on the door comes for an update, I'm going to throw something...while smiling and calm, of course. Never, and I mean *never,* let them see you sweat. I learned how to do this even when a director—or a father—throws something, and I preach that to all my fledgling artists. Did I mention the hot soup was now melting the mortician's wax over her eyebrows? After soup, she had to make an important text. During the entire run of the production, Darcy's main focus was planning her reality show. Lots of phone conversations, a couple of calls from her former husband Danny, her *"wasband."* He was adamantly opposed to having their sons exposed in the new TV series. Having Cooper and Colt's involvement on camera for the world to stare at was a heated debate between them. Impressive, Danny: you're such a good daddy. I wondered what you were like as a life partner. I pondered this question after your acceptance award speech for your last television series when you related the experience to a surreal acid trip. But still, I loved the way you talked to Darcy, and your opinions on your sons' welfare. I deemed you sane. So, who was she texting at this late hour? Was it Danny, her nanny, her father, or was it someone in the reality show production office? Why, no. The texting was to her assistant Sho...who was sitting right next to her. Silly me. I should have guessed. Together they were giggling and texting nonsensical nothingness while I was melting inside, just like her eyebrows.

Moving on to the next crisis, I mean actress: Lillian, the co-lead role with Darcy. She reminded me of a young Barbra Streisand: her mannerisms, her endless exceptional talents, and her intelligence—that nose. Forget about Darcy slow cooking; we needed all hands in the kitchen. Lillian had a horrible rash, located on her lower face and mouth on the right side of the camera frame. I put in a 9-1-1 to my top dermatologist, Pam. Oh, yeah, and get the camera depart-ment in here, discreetly of course, because—hello—you can't hide raised bumpy skin. As a builder, wouldn't I consider using sand paper on her face and, as an architect, a different foundation? I don't possess magical powers, so in that case I needed to improvise. Oh... and let's have a heart-to-heart with your lead actor, Vinny Reyes, because you two will be kissing. Right? Lillian was mortified. She wanted to be airbrushed. No close-ups. Film from the left side of the camera frame. Fix it in post (meaning the edits done after produc-tion). Trista, please tell everyone it's...impetigo. "Okay, Lillian, I will do it but, well...isn't impetigo contagious?"

Darcy and Lillian weren't the only ones out of control. So were the diseases. We had Jason Pink in a cameo appearance for one shooting day. He's a real-life porn star nicknamed "Horn Dog" and has real-life issues growing from his lower lip, as in the kind it's hushed taboo to discuss. Can you hear me in my very quiet voice? When I say...herpes? It was my department's routine for each actor to have a customized kit with makeup, powder, brushes, and disposable essentials like tissues, Q-tips, and sponges. That kit is labeled with their character name and we take it to set for their final touch-ups. We didn't do that for Horn Dog. He entered the makeup trailer. We did our usual meet and greet. I assessed his too-many-to-count hairy, diseased damages and concluded at warp speed we would forego inviting him to sit in the chair. Let's not address the "*eye cookies*," and let's not mess with the beard that starts from inside—and I mean deep inside—his nose. No offers today to give one of my original "*nose pops.*" Yep, I waved and said, "You're good. See you on set." It was my plan to keep it...real. It's one scene. What could possibly go wrong? When the announce-ment of "last looks" is barked, we will go in and say, "Makeup clear." Plan A was in motion. No need to touch the Horn Dog, and the directors would be none the wiser.

We in the movie biz are allowed the unique pleasure of being transported from our base, which for my department is from our trailer, to the set in a passenger van. I've had projects where I'd go from back home to base camp. It's so relaxing to have a driver. It's a perk that I'm quite grateful for. Except—and there was always an exception—when you hear, over the two-way radio drivers carry inside the van, "Makeup, makeup, we need makeup." If someone wants to get ahold of Beckie in the food services department, they yell out her name, not "Kitchen! Kitchen!" Or if they are looking for the director, they don't holler, "Director! Director!" They would address them by their first or last name. Now why is it that—and this happens on every frickin' job I've ever had—they don't ask for a makeup artist by name? In this case it was Amy, who was loading into the transport van when she got the 9-1-1. "Makeup, hustle to set." It appeared there was a problem, Houston.

On occasion, and I'm going off script here but bear with me, I have this strange little issue. I have an annoying chronic tickle in my left nostril, and if this decides to drip when I'm in the presence of another, I touch the top left nostril with my knuckle. Nonchalantly, knuckle to nostril. Slowly. I prefer not to dab with a tissue because then it looks like I have a cold. I don't want the talent to think I'm dishing out transferable germs. I'm a germaphobe builder, after all. Before I touch anyone, I sanitize my hands and make it a point that they see me doing it. So why, seconds before camera was to roll, was there green snot all caught up in Horn Dog's beard, starting at his nostrils and ending in Deadhorse, Alaska? How did he not feel the first little dribble, let alone the snot gushing from his nose? Why not wipe it on his sleeve like any kid...I mean man? Amy doesn't have a kit for him— remember plan A. Wave and smile. No touching Horn Dog. Amy was now quickly changing gears and wrestling with a plan B. Where was her set bag with the tissue on the outside for community crew use and the multitude of supplies? Ah...found it. Oh no, the tissue wasn't replenished before it was sent to set. No tissue. She grabbed the only thing available at the moment: Q-tips. Yep. She did quick nose and beard swirls faster than an ice skating performer doing triple spins. Here is an important news flash for any of you considering going into the field of makeup artistry: run far away. We always hear the comment, "Oh, you have such a glamorous job." Well, we pick nose boogers and yesterday I clipped ear hair, and next I need to lint roll your crotch. Yes, this job is so glamorous.

We had a large cast on that movie. One morning we had a slew of actors for a porn scene in which they all showed lots of skin, and of course, very little primp time. This was low budget. Time is money. How best to get them through makeup...in lightning speed? Line them up from lightest to darkest skin. Let's airbrush. The first one up was Warren. Warren was pleasant and witty, dashed with unassuming good looks. Applying the lightest shade of makeup into the cup of the air gun, spray down the first. Add a few darker drops and move on. I had my assistants powdering the actors and applying glamour with lashes and lipstick to the actresses. The last actress for me to airbrush was the darkest skin-toned. Being my professional self, I kept my eyes focused straight ahead and only on skin. My last actress, Christy, hired only because she slept with one of the producers, wasn't *completely* naked. I'm glad she was last. Her strapped-on dildo blinded me, and I missed Warren's grand nude entrance. He did an experiment to see how much excitement he could muster by arriving to set full Monty. Moments before, he asked my lovely makeup assistant Emily if she doubled as a "fluffer." Emily is proficient in makeup and skincare and she gives a stellar mani-pedi quick as a bunny, but it's not what Warren had in mind. Even though she has a long résumé, "fluffer" is not on it. Her response was a big, fat, "Hell, no." He fluffed on his own and got an X-rated rise from crew and cast.

During the course of filming, Darcy and I *slowly* worked into a rhythmic, arranged understanding. She took her time and I worked balls to the wall. There were days when she insisted on doing her own hair. Her bangs had a mind of their own. Who better to tame them than Darcy herself? Her forehead fringe was on the C-team. They didn't want to be on the varsity squad. I wondered if there was a personality parallel. Darcy and I took lots of pictures together, both smiling into the camera. I'm forever changed on the underlying meanings of seemingly happy behind-the-scenes crew and cast photos.

After filming, Lillian got married as a virgin, and something went terribly awry. They divorced after a few short months.

Warren is still conducting life experiments. He flaunts his ability to swallow multiple hot dogs whole and hires his own hecklers in his stand-up comedy shows.

And what about Horn Dog? Well, for $10 you can dial 1-800-TALK-TO-ME and ask him about his pimp and ho parties. Yeah, he is the host.

Danny completely unraveled. I watched him during a televised interview, rambling, ranting, and chain-smoking. He wasn't alone. He had two new girlfriends helping him take a deep nosedive to the bottom of the celebrity gene pool. Shoots the hell out of my belief in Danny's parental saneness. And his *waswife*, Darcy Black, built a long, 16-episode season with her father and kids.

Like most builders, you finish and you move on, even if the home-owners don't praise your work. My improvised house in the hurricane landed, and safely.

# Illusionist

Sometimes when my back is against the wall, I need to pull a rabbit out of my hat.

*Lonely Hearts* took place in the late 1940s. This movie depicts the true story of two ruthless convicted killers, Martha Beck and Raymond Fernandez. Their plots took advantage of lovelorn war widows who answered the personal ads. They tricked the lonely widows into falling for Ray, who described himself as a "Latin lover." A money scam ensued to cheat them out of their life savings, and then the women were viciously murdered. "Ray" and "Martha," the evil duo, were portrayed by Salma Hayek and Jared Leto.

The filming took place mostly in Florida. There were also shots in LA and then on to New York along with Sing Sing Penitentiary. After the film wrapped and editing began, they realized some additional scenes were needed to tie up some loose ends and make the film flow better in a few transitional areas.

This is where I came in. I was hired to be Jared Leto's personal artist for one day of shooting.

I studied Jared's makeup and hair for continuity with his character, "Ray." It's so important that no one notices any dissimilarities or distractions, especially in these particular scenes with a new artist on board. It's imperative he looks exactly the same. I observed the minimal makeup. He had a receding, balding forehead with a brunette hairpiece placed at ear level. The production company gave me his hairpiece in advance.

Several months had elapsed since the initial main shooting had finished. On the day of my shoot for the additional scenes, I wasn't given the customary makeup trailer, but I had a suite inside a beautiful hotel. I was in awe of this richly historic hotel built in 1914.

I was excited to meet Mr. Leto. He took on challenging roles in movies I admired. *The Thin Red Line* was nominated for seven Oscars, and he had supporting roles in both James Mangold's *Girl, Interrupted* and in David Fincher's cult classic, *Fight Club*.

I glanced around the lobby, looking for a "Ray" look-alike without his hairpiece. The ambiance was warmly lit, with a fireplace and extraordinary features like genuine gold leaf around the hearth. This was a perfect location to film this era. We were shooting one of the scenes where "Ray" was fine-dining his innocent victims. I couldn't find Jared.

During Jared's time off from filming with Salma Hayak he'd gone on tour with his band, Thirty Seconds to Mars. Music had been his initial draw to LA before the acting bug bit him. He is the lead vocalist, guitarist, bassist, and played keyboards along with his brother, Shannon.

The producer on this project found me wandering and led me to Jared, who was sitting comfortably in an oversized elegant chair by the fireplace. Time is money, no wandering allowed.

"Hi, Trista? I'm Jared." No. Must be a mistake. I felt a wild ride coming on. This man who says he is "Jared" has long blue-black hair. No wonder I missed seeing "Ray." He isn't "Ray." This was not computing in my mind, with the continuity pictures and the video clips I had been studying. Where was his short, balding brown hair? Is he an illusion?

I'm all about developing a character with an actor and director. Many changes are possible with latex, lace wigs, and shaving, color, whatever it takes. However, normally, it's at the front end of a project and I'm given time. Transitioning talent into the on-screen persona with makeup and hair is extremely rewarding. But now, toes are tapping, fingers are pointing as the clock is ticking. It's all about continuity and making him look the same for a movie he had already finished. Where was the proper communication and notification so I could prepare? This was one of those moments in my career when I wished I had magical powers or my name was Jeannie and I lived in a bottle, or I was Samantha and with one twitch of my good witch nose the impossible become very possible.

The upside to this moment was that we were shooting at night. I like working when it's dark. The downside is that it's at night. It's not during business hours. Where is an open beauty supply store if you need hair color, heaven forbid? Oh, and I'm going to need a hair/makeup trailer that sports a sink to rinse out said color. Perhaps there is no upside.

Going from bluish black to brunette hair is quite a process. Imagine taking a dark color crayon and then layering with other colors to make it appear lighter. I think not.

This was going to take a colorizing hair specialist. With a firestorm of frenzied phone calls from me and the rest of the local community, we seized upon a willing hair professional to take on our emergency quest. She had a studio in close proximity to our location.

Jared understood the quandary. He explained how he had also tweezed his hair before the filming to eliminate hair and get into the "Ray" forehead baldness. Jared was calm, patient, and a willing participant. Boom...I found the upside.

Within hours, director Todd Robinson, "T-Rob," was breathing fire down my neck, cursing. I was costing production tens of thousands in delays and the dollar number was growing by the second. At that very moment I wished I could wave a hocus pocus wand. Where is my rabbit?

T-Rob was good at barking orders...a US Navy Submarine Corps veteran who had been awarded the Navy Commendation Medal for lifesaving. He also served as a Poseidon Missile Tech...and yes, I was shaking in my boots.

T-Rob and his lead actor Jared Leto shared a common interest: both musicians and singers. Surely of all people, T-Rob would've been aware of his radical musician changing-hair possibilities?

We cut Jared's hair and shaved his forehead to give him a receding hairline. I only say "we" because I watched the colorist, Sonna Brado. She did a color application, shampoo, color application, shampoo, and after endless repeats, we got the color close enough. I was then able to put on the hairpiece and Jared Leto, the musician with blue-black hair, had turned into "Ray," the 1940s villain with a brown half-shaved head and a hairpiece.

With the additional help of my hair guru extraordinaire, Mike Meyers, we styled a sea of our featured women answering the lovelorn ads to meet "Ray." We were ready to rock and roll. I guess I'm an illusionist, in a non-musical kind of way.

After Jared played "Ray," he won an Academy Award for *Dallas Buyers Club.* I was in awe of his excellence in portraying a transgender person with AIDS and I'm sure our exercise with illusions was just a warm up.

# Poker Player

*SPOKANE, WASHINGTON, My hometown*

James Woods has been nominated for and won every acting award imaginable, even some I never knew existed. What the hell is a Golden Apple? KCFCC: does it mean Kentucky clam-fried chicken chow-down? Independent Spirit: go James go? Golden Satellite: is he rated out of this world? The list is endless: American Television, Critics Choice, Cable Ace, CFCA, Maverick, Sierra, NSFCC, OFTA, Magnolia, Role Model Award, and then of course the biggies. You live under a rock if you aren't familiar with Primetime Emmys, Daytime Emmys, SAG, Golden Globe, and Academy. Actually, what hasn't he won? That might be of more interest.

Woods usually plays dark, intense characters, such as a sadistic killer in *The Onion Field,* and a serial murderer in *Killer: A Journal of*

*Murder.* His current lead role was in the TV series *The Shark.* When James arrived to work on a small film, he instantly changed accommodations to the modest Oxford Suites because he'd brought his little doggie. His personal pet wasn't welcome at the historic upscale Davenport, where every big actor gets the red carpet rolled out in Spokane. Forgoing Ritz for a more humble abode, James put his pet's well-being before his own personal comforts.

However, my judge and jury were still out. What was under the hood? Would he be a respected murderer? I'm always curious about the behavior of the man behind the characters he plays. In this small movie he was cast as a co-conspirator to kill the president. Hell, if anyone can get away with it...have you seen those awards?

Inside the makeup trailer, I had my appointed actors and they didn't include Mr. Woods. His makeup artist, Angel, was working in the station next to me. The focus with James was getting his eyebrows just right. It was a daily fuss fest.

"No, Angel, can't you see the right brow needs to be just a tad higher? Here, give me your brush. See? Let's add a little color. Yes...great...okay...you got it, Angel?" I was relieved I wasn't his artist. Because, no, I couldn't see his right brow needed to be higher.

It wasn't until several weeks into our shooting schedule that I became aware of Wood's poker credits. Now this was something to write home about. He had memorable roles in gambling-themed films such as *Casino* and *The Gambler.* And off camera, James is a famously popular celeb in esteemed poker circuits like the World Poker Tour and the World Series of Poker, along with endorsing the poker book entitled *Little Green Book,* written by respected player Phil Gordon. He cashed dozens of times in major events and finished deep in numerous prestigious tournaments. Woods also appeared on the show *Celebrity Poker* and he and his brother Michael often played online at "Hollywood Poker."

During one of our days off, Mr. Woods (or Jimmy, as I called him), along with some of the producers, arranged a crew and cast no-limit poker tournament. It was held inside a small hair salon conveniently located next to the production office. Tables were brought in along with eager volunteers to deal, who wanted to meet or had hopes to have one-on-one time with the movie actors. This was my first poker game and my naiveté was soaring. I could go home after just one hand! How embarrassing. I understood there was no limit on a bet. If I bet all my chips, I risked everything. Are the other crew members feeling this way or is this just a girl thing? I had very little invested except my time and a little money. I had absolutely no reason to be nervous with this invitation except that I was in the presence of a grand poker enthusiast, James Woods. I had no expectations, only pleasant thoughts of my card experiences with my grandpa, who had long passed, and I couldn't help but wander back in time.

Asa (so fittingly pronounced ACE-a) taught me how to play pinochle. He was adored in his community of Priest River, Idaho, not only for plowing out the families during the wicked winters, but also for his uncanny card-playing abilities. You would often find me proudly tucked in close beside him so I could watch his card-shark skills. His buddies played pinochle while smoking cigars. Asa always puffed on his pipe. To this day, I reflect on his unique sweet tobacco aroma. Still lingering. It evokes a warm fuzzy feeling deep within me, like the smell of percolating coffee over a wood fire during Priest Lake camping trips, at the first morning light. Certain scents stay forever.

Grandpa played a type of pinochle called racehorse. There were four players at each table with your partner sitting directly across. I never had doubts he would take all the tricks. Asa was a phenom in pinochle. The good old boys he played with flinched when he often announced, "I'm shooting the moon. I'm taking 'em all...reaping... and making you all weep." For years I watched him win.

One Saturday, Asa grabbed me and whisked us into a pinochle tournament and it was *me* sitting across the table. I was his partner. His old buddies were snickering and pointing toward me.

"Whatcha got going here, Asa?" I was very conscious of the strange looks coming my way. Did they feel slighted that Asa didn't ask any of them to be his partner? Is this a girl thing? My grandpa had no doubts in his choice. He had a lot of confidence in my play. I had developed an intuition for passing the best four cards. His peeps quieted down when we won the tournament. I was quite an anomaly to those old geezers. I was 10.

As I become an adult, I continued to play card games such as gin rummy, solitaire, hearts, but I found this poker gig was completely different from anything I have ever played, even pinochle. True, most of the players here in this makeshift card room are men. I'm trying to follow along, take it all in. I know I don't want to go home yet, so to say the words "all in" could be sudden death.

During our first break in the action, Mr. Jimmy Woods took me aside. Huddled by him listening to his hushed voice, I felt like he was a quarterback and I was a mistake-ridden rookie.

"Hey, listen up." Jimmy continued to instruct me. "I want you to make it to the final table with me, but you clearly need to change your play. We are among amateurs who will call, limp, and want to see every flop. Hell, I just hit Broadway and lost on the river." The *Tristinary* wasn't going to be of use in this situation. I suddenly had the need for a poker glossary. Limp...flop...huh?

Jimmy continued. "So, are you with me, here? You're going to play the opposite. Okay? Conservative. It boils down to position. Don't bet when you're out of position. If you are under the gun, even a small pair needs to be folded. If your cards equal 20, raise big."

Twenty was a significant number to James. He started dating Ashley Madison when she was 20, 40 years his junior, and left her when she was 26, to start dating a felon, Kristin Baugness, and yes, his new girlfriend was 20. "Okay...any questions, Trista?"

While the unfamiliar rules were still swimming in my newbie mind, I started to mumble, "What is the right position?" I thought twice. I was curious to know if he had bedded a few of the woman actresses in this film and I didn't want to put myself in a position to discuss positions.

I went back to my table rehearsing Jimmy's rules in my head. The game took on a slow pace while waiting for the right cards and in the right rotation to play.

While I patiently waited for those precious pairs equaling 20, my thoughts flashed back to another time when I was the card quarterback as a single mama. I was continually playing card games with my two little dotkins. Dotkin or dot is the Tristanary word for daughter. Blackjack was our favorite, not really age-appropriate. I justified it though. Good for their math skills? We had meager wealth. We used breakfast cereal. Moneyless. Perfect.

"Trista... Trista...*Trista*. Check or bet?" The dealer snapped me from daydreaming of my dots and back into the present game. I wonder what the winnings are for this poker tournament. Are they more valuable than breakfast cereal?

I took Jimmy's advice. When I was one of the first players to act, out of position, I folded my small pairs...very reluctantly. They were so pretty and they didn't come around often. When I had a big pocket pair like tens or QQ that equaled 20, I politely set most of my chips in. More experienced players shove, flick, spill their chips in. No, I neatly set them in the middle; a dead giveaway of a rookie player. I learned Broadway wasn't a big-time stage show Jimmy Woods was going to perform on a river, it was A, K, Q, J, 10. Hours later I indeed made it to the final table. There were six other players, including Jimmy. It was inconceivable that a few disciplined rules could help me surpass the field, but three players busted out which left three players remaining. Our last hand, ironically, was when Jimmy and

I both shoved all our chips in at the same time along with the last player. We both lost the hand to the ultimate winner.

"Tied for second. Not bad, Trista," Jimmy said proudly, like a quarterback whose rookie just made an unlikely touchdown.

After that first game with Woods in the hair salon I continued to be a student of poker. I found no-limit to be a fascinating study of human behavior, and very helpful to master some knowledge of people's reactions for the makeup trailer. I remember an actress who paid full airfare for a wig to have its own first-class seat. She upped the ante and I knew the wig was a game-changer requiring a specialized handler.

My poker skills evolved as I gained more experience by playing at a local casino. I incorporated new sets of rules. Ultimately knowing the other players at the table and reading with my gut was an unteachable intuition starting back with my grandpa.

While I worked with Ray Liotta, before his current role with J-Lo on *Shades of Blue* and well after his role in *Goodfellas*, he had me set up poker games for him on our days off. The casino was thrilled to have a celebrity playing with their regulars. Liotta was relatively new to poker, so while we were prepping in the makeup trailer he would shoot me questions from our game the night before.

"Trista, why did you push all in when I raised on the button?"

"I knew you were bluffing, Ray."

Each time we played, Liotta lost a little money, but every time I overheard conversations at the casino, the amount got bigger.

"Hey, I played with Ray Liotta—you know, the movie star—and I won a thousand dollars off of him."

A few months after we filmed, Ray's losses were in the tens of thousands. It was like the fish they caught just kept getting bigger until it was Moby Dick.

Playing with Jimmy had significantly upped my game. The summer of 2006, I was in Vegas waiting to play in my first World

Macklemore (Ben Haggerty) and I taking a break while I create '70s makeup and hair for the music video "Downtown," seen over 44 million times on YouTube.

Playful drama with me and lead actress Amber Heard on the movie set of *The Ward*. #HurtMeBeforeIHurtYou

Tea tree oil isn't really necessary for Christian Slater to give one of his traditional stellar performances (but it can help!).

Before *Game of Thrones*, there was *Knights of Badassdom*. Peter Dinklage is waiting for me to apply his special effects makeup.

Academy Award winner Cuba Gooding Jr. is my inspiration to add a new word to my Tristinary: cubaconfusa.

Last looks on the super chill birthday boy, Snoop Dogg.

"Katelyn" lies under the tarp while she waits for her rainbow to kick in. (Read more about Katelyn on page 158.)

Ray Liotta and I swap poker stories during a late night of shooting.

Michael Gladis and I celebrate after I spontaneously recreated his famous *Mad Men* beard with yak hair.

Who's the dummy? #JamesCarpenter #Thriller

This farm baby didn't require anything from my makeup bag.

This actor is so patient while I airbrush stitches on his belly.

Every girl needs hair extensions to accentuate her mane, and Blondie is no exception.

This was an unbearably hot film day. We pumped oxygen between takes for the sweating actor behind the fur.

A day off and I'm in my happy place on a Maui beach.

Actress, producer, and famous author of *Mommie Dearest*, Christina Crawford is one of my oldest clients. We are in New York debuting her Broadway musical. #WeHaveWonAwards

Taci and I in Greenbluff, Washington, where I had just finished makeup for a wedding. She's no longer a participant in Bring Your Daughter To Work Day. #WeddingCrasher

Erin Cummings and I are traveling to the set after I created a 1960s makeup look for the upcoming film, *Language Arts*.

My sisteress and bestie Amy with actor Jared Harris, known for his roles on *Mad Men* and *Chernobyl*.

The leading stars in my life are Lindsey, Taci, Joshua, Avery, Landon, Emersyn, and Conner. We love to get away to Idaho.

I reflect on my life as I watch the sunset on the Snoqualmie River in Western Washington.

Series of Poker tournament. I had won a satellite tournament giving me the money to buy into the prestigious event. My dot was with me. To kill some time, I got into a cash game. Taci sat behind me and watched intently. After a few hours, my dot proclaimed, "I'm ready!"

"You're ready for what?" I asked.

"I'm going to buy in," my innocent child stated.

"Oh, no, you don't. You could lose all your money in just one hand."

Off she went to the cashier cage to buy her chips. She was on a wait list and when it was her turn, the floor manager seated her—at my table. This was so wrong. Wasn't there a separate children's table, like at the big family Thanksgiving meal? When did she get to be an adult? Now I was the Jimmy-quarterback rallying her in a whispered voice. I took her aside.

"Taci, there are some new players at this table since you were here observing. The older Asian woman plays big hands. She will push you until you bleed or cry for mercy. Don't get tangled with her, okay?"

"Yes, Mama." Firsthand, and Taci was under the gun, or first to act behind the dealer button. I expected her to fold her cards and warm up a bit. Yeah, no. She placed a bet based on her two hole cards. All the remaining men folded, except the older Asian woman I warned Taci about; she raised with a large bet. The sweat pooled under my always-stay-poker-calm demeanor. Surely Taci will get scared and fold. Taci called. My heart leaped. The dealer displayed the three community cards called the flop. It's down to two players, and Taci was the first to act. I'm going ballistic inside my head...check, Taci, check. Taci bets.

Oh. My. *God*. The Asian woman raised...Taci called. The dealer revealed the Fourth Street or the turn. Taci bets, out of position, the cardinal sin for new players in Jimmy's book. The Asian woman raised the bet...and why shouldn't she? She wanted all my daughter's money, but my baby needs new shoes. Taci matched her bet with a call. The last card in poker is the river. Taci looked to me. Finally, for the first time, my dot hesitated. "What should I do?"

"You waited to ask me until now? Check." Please go find a children's table. The female opponent checked too. I didn't see that coming. Based on what I saw on the board, there were no straight or flush possibilities. The Asian woman confidently flipped up her cards to reveal her strong three-of-a-kind, trips. Well, it beats any pair or two pair. Taci reluctantly turned over her hand. The highly anticipated winner was unveiled. The dealer pushed all the chips to Taci. I was in shock. The rest of the players were stunned. She had a full house. The table buzzed with comments for Taci. "Why did you check if you knew you had the nuts?" asked one of the male players.

"Well, because my mama told me to."

"Whoa...that's your mama?" Taci gave me the look. Again. The man continued. "You look like sisters."

My daughters and I get that a lot. Makes me feel fantastic. Makes Taci and Lindsey shake their heads. My girls always give me this look like, *really?* The player next to Taci squealed. "Is this the first time you've played cards?"

"No, I've played before, not with money, but with Cheerios!" The table roared in laughter and one gentleman fell off his chair.

After I successfully pulled Taci off the table, I stowed her away to a safer activity, window shopping, while I moved on to the real reason I was in Vegas. It was time for my first World Series poker event.

I taxied over to the Rio Casino where all the World Series events were held. The driver dropped me off at a separate doorway behind and around back of the main entrance. The carpet was red leading from the taxi stand up the stairs. Interesting observation...was the red carpet a symbol of a parallel universe? Celebrity award shows to poker showdowns? I was in complete awe of the opulent decor leading to the registration. I was overwhelmed with the presence of greatness. The distinguished poker gods had portraits imposing in on us from the grand hallways. Doyle Brunson, who reminded me of my grandpa, was one of my favorite past winners. Johnny Chen, Phil Hellmuth (the "Poker Brat"), along with Chris Ferguson and dozens of smug faces pictured with a stack of their winning chips. I was still relatively new at this sport. I had absolutely no comparison to these impressive professionals. No way in hell I'm ready for the grand-daddy of all poker tournaments, the main event, but today, I'm entering into a much smaller World Series of Poker game. There were so many contests from which to choose, and some I had never heard of: H.O.R.S.E, Razz, Low-ball. Sounds like a carnival. Well, it sort of is. I'm sure I will be entertained and taken on a ride.

I located the cashier's room where a long Disneyland-style back-and-forth rope separated the players in line waiting to pay. When I finally got to the cage, I forked over my free ticket from the satellite I had previously won in Spokane. I was given two white cards. One was a receipt and the other the dealer copy. On the card was stated the ballroom, table number, and seat, which is randomly computer selected. I was glad I arrived early. It was overwhelming locating the specified ballroom and swimming through the sea of tables. Seated were mostly all men wearing dark sunglasses. I was definitely feeling like a fish out of water.

When I landed at my destination, I handed in my dealer copy along with my driver's license to verify that yes, the two matched. Now if I can continue to get cards to match, I'm in business. I kept my head down and was focused only on my cards. I was oblivious to my surroundings, which completely signified my lack of confidence.

Several hands were dealt before the uncomfortable fog started lifting. I noticed a unique and familiar voice at my table, from the gentleman directly to my left. I don't recognize the face at all. "Hey, are you behaving over there, Michael?" I heard the same voice, but from a neighboring gentleman with his back to me at the next table over. Is there an echo in here? Is the pressure getting to me? Well,

well, the mystery unfolded. Jimmy Woods stood and turned from his table to address his younger brother Michael, who was sitting next to me. What are the chances? Thousands of players at this tournament and I'm in between the Woods brothers? Unbelievable.

"I will see your cynicism, Michael, and I raise you some badass." Watching Jimmy and Michael interact during the tournament with cheeky humor, deep respect, and love was immensely fun. I no longer cared about winning. I enjoyed their kinship!

All three of us busted out around the same time. Jimmy and Michael were swapping bad beat stories on what should've happened if the opponents had played their hands correctly. I guess those donkeys didn't get a copy of *The Rules According to Jimmy* book. It's a familiar song ringing throughout every poker conversation; the walk of shame after losing; the explanation to the consoling friend on why you're not still winning.

We parted ways in the grandiose poker hallway. It was the last time I was to ever see Michael Woods. When Michael returned home he had a fatal heart attack. He was only 49. This was my first World Series and it was Michael's last. It haunts me.

I continue to play each summer in Vegas at the World Series of Poker. I don't have a poker handle like "Phil the Poker Brat" or "Mike the Mouth." I haven't seen Jimmy again. He has taken a very long break from the World Series after his brother's untimely death.

Several years later I worked on a project with Danielle Panabaker. I was reliving my Jimmy poker story in the makeup trailer. I described my mentor, James Woods, as my card-playing idol. My actress in the chair pulled out her phone. "Hey, I'm friends with Jimmy." My actress was excited to text him. "Hey, James, I'm here with Trista—and she says hello!"

Woods was quick to reply. "I take full credit for creating that poker monster."

I've enjoyed a small amount of success. I was featured in a local televised tournament and have been interviewed by Fox and ESPN. I was also written about in *Western Gamblers Magazine.* I've won countless satellites to buy in to the World Series.

I was invited to play in a highly publicized local poker tournament with a large prize pool rewarded. I bumped into an acquaintance, Bruno, on one of my breaks and he said he had been watching me play. My poker night ended when I went all in with pocket kings. I fantasized I'd be getting paid when my opponent showed pocket 10s, but the river took me out when an unlikely 10 popped to give him trips over my pair. As I was walking away, Bruno asked if he could buy me a drink and I told him no, I was meeting with my sister. I had a cocktail with my sister and her husband, and kissed them goodnight. Bruno swooped in with a drink. I didn't want to be impolite, so I said, "Cheers," took a swig, and continued on to meet up with another group of friends. After a few minutes I was confused. My body was in slow motion. I became paralyzed and collapsed. My daughter, Taci, was called before I was in the ambulance. My dot arrived at the emergency room before I did. A chaplain was waiting for her because the paramedics had needed to pull over to conduct life-saving treatments. After several days in the ICU, the hospital administrators asked me what I thought happened. They were unable to conduct a drug test because the treatments they'd administered interfered with accurate results. I cringe at the fact that I could have been led away by Bruno the lion, never to be seen again. The security tapes were erased before I could request them. That was standard procedure after a week.

My last tournament entered was in the summer of 2014. Out of 909 players, I took 43rd. I actually tried to talk the 44th-place finisher to swap with me as we walked to the prize table, because I have a thing with fours. It's my favorite number, along with my dots, but after the long card marathon we both just finished, he wasn't paying attention due to exhaustion. He smiled and motioned. "Ladies first."

I think I want a new favorite number...one. I will never have a World Class poker status like Mr. James Woods. However, I will always be grateful for his mentorship, along with that of my grandpa.

# Boss

Everyone has a personal stylist of choice to frequent for hair maintenance. My go-to favorite is Mike Meyers (his comedic ability may be
on point...however, I can assure you he is not the well-known *Austin
Powers* Mike Myers). My Meyers is a handsome Asian gay man who
my daughter, Lindsey, turned me on to. He is extraordinary with
color, cut, and sometimes even more importantly, conversation.

Often times, out of unfortunate necessity, I become a hairstylist.
Mostly I just place the hair. A wispy strand not behaving? I can tame
it. Locks need curling? I can usually do it. Match continuity from day
five with day 25? No problem. Need a haircut? Prayers commence.
Scissors and sizzling tools shouldn't be left in my control. It's definitely not my forte. I will shamefully throw myself under the bus
and admit I once burned Lainie Kazan's forehead with a curling

iron, and just recently singed my own bangs and was forced to cut out the burned pieces and then hide for three weeks. There are plenty of great hairstylists out there, and I'm clearly not one of them.

When I became a boss and did hiring for my own departments, it was only natural to employ Mike Meyers, my personal stylist. As a boss, it was important I laid out for him the daring task at hand. Meyers was to develop character tresses to complement all the roles in the movie, while simultaneously schmoozing the actors in order to build a trusting rapport. Meyers had it all: skills and personality to answer any celebrity challenge. On *Home of the Brave,* Meyers got radioed to blast onto set. The entire camera department was fixated on Meyers as he entered. Christina Ricci's bangs had fallen forward onto her forehead and created a distraction while she was delivering her lines.

"I don't want this to ever happen again!" said the cinematographer. I had instructed Meyers on day one never to use hairspray on Christina, at her request. We glanced at each other, defeated but knowingly, and mutually agreed there was no other option. He sprayed her fringe behind her ears to keep it in place. If Christina was sitting at his salon chair right now her hair would be flowing free; it would be good enough to be in a L'Oréal commercial, but there is quite a contrast between camera hair and everyday hairstyles. "Thanks, Mark," the cinematographer dismissed Meyers as he looked around. Is he talking to me? I guess "Mark" is better than being called "Hair." Meyers ignored him.

The next day, Meyers was behind the monitor watching Christina's hair. If it didn't change, I told him, he wouldn't need to go in and hairspray. He could make Christina, me, and the cinematographer happy. Hours later, and Christina's hair was still holding. The cinematographer looked at Meyers. "Did you do anything?"

"No," said Meyers. He felt as long as her hair stayed in place, he wouldn't "do anything."

As a boss, sometimes it's not about instructing but consoling and supporting your employees. Meyers used me as a sounding board to vent his understandable frustrations.

The following week Christina's character was wearing an elegant dress and I suggested Meyers put her hair in a simple and classic French twist. The cinematographer inspected Christina. "Love the hair, who is responsible?"

"I am." I guess Meyers finally hit his "Mark."

Meyers went with the flow, and as a boss, I appreciated that. On another show we had an actress flying in from Brazil and we were planning to put her in Meyers' chair immediately to assess her character in the film and start discussing style.

"In my country, this is how we do it," she would say after every request. Our Brazilian actress had thick, frizzy curls and she wanted a big thicker, frizzier mess, even though it didn't match the character she portrayed. Meyers handled our foreign princess gracefully, and as his boss that's what I look for.

Meyers was continually being pulled in another direction. He had a long list of clients waiting to sit in his chair at his salon—the mark of being too good. I had an immediate need for an entertainment hair guru to supplement Meyer's high demands outside this industry.

I started calling on the union. They had a roster of members to fill openings. Meyers still had my back, and would help me on occasion, but I needed a full-time commitment. "You can cheat on me, Trista; just don't divorce me," said Meyers.

The union suggested Rose. She was pleasant and confident. She drove across the state with her tools in tow. As I worked from my side of the trailer, I watched her bonding with Beckett, her first actor. I could hear friendly chatter and, relieved, I took a deep breath. Then our lead actor suddenly left.

"Trista, can I talk to you?" asked Rose.

Normally, I would never leave my actor in the makeup chair alone, but this wasn't normal. I motioned to Rose and we stepped outside.

"Excuse me, Trista, but how do I color hair? I told Beckett to come back in a few minutes while I set up, but I've never done it."

I grabbed the phone and called Meyers first and the union second.

"Send me another union referral!" I felt like I was a coach calling up a player from the minor farm league to the majors. Can they hit a home run under pressure?

Laura hummed while she worked. Not quietly under her breath, but louder than our music. When is it ever all right to hum?

As a boss, I learned how to get better at firing. Lolly wore high heels and low-cut dresses, despite filming in cow pastures and crawling onto process trailers (a staging platform on wheels typically used to film car scenes).

Next!

Georgie repeatedly stabbed my lead actress on the forehead with the end of her metal teasing comb.

Dave didn't even own combs, so I booked Stella on the next flight. "Do I need to actually touch the hair? Or is it okay if I just use hairspray from a distance?" She was booked on the next return flight.

That's when I started asking for résumés and portfolios. Chelsea had an interesting one. She was an intern I had used years prior and I liked her. She had moved away and gained valuable experience. She sent me her portfolio of her work, and half of it I recognized because it was my work. My intricate special effects she had removed from the actor at wrap.

On to Jonathan. "Don't ask me to do ponytails or braids, Trista," which prompted a desperate call to my dotkin.

"Taci," I pleaded, "I need you to be my pinch hitter. I have a mass of school-kid extras coming through tomorrow needing braids, ponies, barrettes, and headbands."

"Okay, Mama, but do you know why I'm getting my master's degree? Because I want to be anything *but* a hairstylist."

Along came Maggie. We had a meet and greet scheduled with our lead actress. When our talent arrived Maggie didn't say hello, extend her hand, or create eye contact. She ran out of the trailer to take a personal call, and she was always on the phone. As a boss, I can't teach manners.

Louella disappeared whenever we had to wrap our trailer for a location move. Ostensibly her father had been an active military serviceman and she had gone to a different school every year. She had a post-traumatic move disorder.

Next was Gwen, and she had a different disorder. She wouldn't use the honey wagon, our bathroom on wheels. She would drive to the nearest town.

Connie had scheduling conflicts. She wouldn't mention her son was in a baseball game she couldn't possibly miss until he was in the third inning—right before she would abandon me, and I have abandonment issues. Next movie, new crew family, repeat.

Then came Vaughn. He saw the cast list and decided to change careers.

Parker wanted to do something lovely for me. He decided my bangs needed trimming. He wet them down and with one swift chop of the scissors they were gone. They took a month to grow out, but I love hats, anyway. The revolving door of snafus continued.

On a non-union job, I called a local trendy hair studio and recruited a new stylist, Gabby. Unlike Meyers, she didn't have a clientele built yet. It was a good fit. The actors immediately embraced Gabby and I was delighted, until I received a nasty gram from the salon accusing me of stealing their employee. I didn't realize the youngling was under contract. She was an apprentice in exchange for employment at the salon. I was instructed to never step foot on their property, as if I'd pocketed the little blonde thing and shoplifted her right out of their storefront. A little overkill, don't you think? I did return her in the same condition I received her.

I had an assistant who asked for a mirror. Easy, done. As a boss, I provide supplies, but no, she asked for a mirror from the crowd of fans watching the video, and a reporter sniffed out the story and it made news.

On the following gig, I had a hairstylist take three hours to put rollers in our A-list actress' shoulder-length hair, and an hour to take out said rollers—every day.

After the painfully slow stylist, I filmed additional scenes with Demi Moore, and she brought her own hairstylist, Ricky. Curiously, he used drugstore hair products. We were shooting her scene at night in a restaurant with the lighted city landscape as the background. I noticed flyaway pieces sure to distract a viewer. I explained it to Ricky. "Demi was backlit. Her hair will need to be smoothed with product." He completely ignored me and disappeared without addressing the annoyance. I just chalked it up to his need for hearing aids, but could I gift the same ignorance to the camera department when they busted *me* for her hair faux pas? Not so lucky.

A noteworthy encounter was when a stylist had partied the night before and overslept. Because she failed to report, I had to step in and perform. Yes, perform. Jayda was part of the superstar's entourage. She was a buddy with the lead actor since grade school. On our first day, Jayda went into great detail about how she intricately sewed in extra strands of hair at the back of his head to give him a longer, more natural-looking mane. Impressive. I had hair extensions once and Meyers glued them in. Jayda did Preston's hair in the privacy of his trailer, so I never witnessed this painfully long specialized process. On the morning Jayda missed her call time, I panicked. I was forced to be Preston's substitute hair seamstress. I don't sew. I toss my shirts if they need a popped button sewn on.

"Good morning, Preston. Let's get you ready." I didn't want to ask Preston for any instructions. I didn't want him to think I was insanely ignorant, but I was feeling insanely ignorant. Mirror, mirror on the wall, Trista's going to slip and fall. I was digging into his kit for hair, thread, and sewing needles. I pulled out hair attached to clips. Do I sew in these clips, and where is the thread? That looked too simple. Could it be? I fastened one of the clips. "Is that comfortable?" I really wanted to blurt out, "Is that what she does? Just hides rows of clips under your hair?" I turned his chair slightly to the side so he could get a look into the mirror. I braced myself for a look of disdain or befuddlement from Preston and I grasped for ideas to explain an added step to be different from what Jayda did.

"Looks great." Preston nodded with approval, and I continued to add the remaining stashes of hair, bewildered by Jayda's unnecessary drama.

As I returned to my trailer, Amy barred the door. "Tris, do not go in."

"Amy, stop teasing."

"No, I'm serious. Randy is on his way." Randy is a first-class producer and a cool cat. Who better to straighten out a supposed mess?

"Are we being robbed? Guns drawn? Step aside, my dearie." I giggled, but our world was not as we left it. We entered into a frenzied chaos with a small army of uninvited bimbo types, using our hair tools, supplies, and makeup. Jayda finally arrived and pushed me out of the doorway. "Thanks, Jayda, for letting us, like, hang out and, like, use your digs," said one girlie.

"I ran into Preston, and wow, like his hair is like totally rockin'," said another.

"Thanks. That's why I'm late; hand-sewing each piece took me forever." Jayda qualified without even blinking.

Amy raised a brow. Witnessing a person who believed her own lies was eyebrow raising.

"Amy, let's hire celebrity friends. They show up one day as a bystander and the next day they have a walkie and they're giving orders. Surely that will end my predicaments," I whispered.

Amy agreed. "This was a shit show with snobby people. Let's call it a day."

There are advantages of being a boss and receiving employee perks. Producers gave me a break from being a boss with concert tickets to The Boss. The very long winding road to the concert crawled bumper-to-bumper. The journey to this venue seemed painfully excruciating. Why? Because my imprudent gas gauge was reading "E." And it didn't stand for E Street, Bruce Springsteen's band. Booya. What a treat. I'm all in. I gambled when I didn't take the time to stop for fuel, but this was my first trip to Dodger Stadium. Who knew it would be a virtual parking lot of cars snailing their way to the top, and I'd be burning my precious gas fumes? My palms were sweating and my stomach was anxious. I tapped the steering wheel. Shouldn't all you beep peeps be seated? The concert was ready to start. If I ran out of gas, I planned on jumping out and running the rest of the way. I will deal with my stupidity later. Could everyone ignore the idiot car with its flashing lights and pass around me?

Whew—I made it!

I was fully engaged in Bruce's performance. I had completely forgotten about the stress of being a boss and my 16-hour workday on that hot July night. Springsteen was energizing and clearly didn't act his age; full-on delivering, and bringing it each and every song. While rocking to "I'm on Fire," I was certain it was my favorite until he sang "Dancing In the Dark," and I was convinced it was my favorite until he performed "Born to Run," and I went ballistic, which was close to being my mantra driving here. Yeah, "Born to Run," was my ultimate favorite.

The sun was setting and the fans were engrossed, reliving emotional memories with every familiar tune. Swaying. Dancing. Singing.

A powerful awareness washed over me. Instinctively I turned and looked up, slightly above me in the box seats. Our eyes locked. He was a handsome, riveting man. Time. Stood. Still. The movement of the crowd was all one party, engulfed around us, but we were alone. Together. Eye to eye. With Tom Hanks.

Back to work. Hiring a department had its challenges. However, I was on a project where I was given an assistant. The shooting location was the Sunset-Gower Studios, formerly the Columbia Studio lot. I kept taking snapshots of the Hollywood sign on the hillside. It was surreal. This was my new home, and I had a makeup room inside the large studio and also a trailer to be transported to our next location. I was thrilled to meet my new assistant, Tammy, because she was an award winning makeup artist. What can I learn from her? What products are in her kit? Will she be anything like my favorite sidekick, Amy? My excitement was building as I set up the makeup room.

"Hey, Tammy!" I said. She walked away from me, pulled out a chair, and plopped down. "Let's get something straight. I'm not here to work, Trista, in any way, shape, or form. I'm here for a paycheck. You got it?"

"Oh, I'm...huh."

"I'm friends with the producer so you can't fire me. Basically just pretend I'm not here." Tammy opened her romance paperback and started reading. Snap.

I've seen artists who don't do their fair share. Once while working on a musical television show, I was just one of a dozen makeup artists in the green room. We had 30 superstar musicians on set, but only a few artists followed through to do last looks. The amplified telecom kept requesting makeup help, but to no avail. The other artists disappeared. At the end of the night, when the performers came through to have makeup removed, it was the same deal: a skeleton crew. But at the time of wrap when we filled out our time sheets and turned them in for signatures, surprise! All the makeup artists were accounted for.

The following week I said goodbye to the Hollywood sign that peered down on our Glover Boulevard studio lot, and our carnival moved locations to a residential area. The street was lined up on both sides with grip trucks, craft services, catering, electrical, star trailers, and production crews. Our set was located at the far end of the development, inside a home at the end of a gated cul-de-sac. No trailers were allowed inside the gate because of the camera angles. Golf carts were used to cart equipment because of the steepness of the hill and the distance from the base camp. I had four actors for whom I'd be in charge. It could have been two actors if you divided it by two, but Tammy wasn't going to help.

"Hey, Tammy and Trista, I want to show you a change to the schedule." Joshua handed us both a copy of the daily sides. I didn't tell him every day he was wasting paper on Tammy. She was using her sides as a bookmark.

"We are going to shoot the flashback in between the two present-day scenes so the camera doesn't have to move. That means all four actors need to be in the present-day look and then we need to shoot the flashback where they were 20 years younger and then the very next scene back to present-day." Tammy closed her book. "Impossible, Joshua, the camera will be waiting on us and it's not going to save time."

I'm following the facts, that I'm being asked to change four different characters four different looks, three different times, but I was stuck on Tammy's use of the word "us."

"It would help if we move everything into the house," said Joshua. Again, I can't get past "us." "I will send you a golf cart."

With the new development of an impossible request for me to perform solo, I was sure Tammy would hit the pause button on book number three and assist me. When I'm on set struggling, won't she feel guilty?

I gathered up my station and loaded the wigs, mustaches, and all the kits to make my characters look younger, and sat on the curb.

Where was the golf cart and will Tammy show up? I saw lots of carts buzzing around, but they were all in use.

What kind of boss am I? An inept overworked peon who looks like a Sherpa. I'm a boss of myself if I'm leading no one, and on that job it started and ended with me, myself, and I. *A familiar feeling, since the age of three.*

My dilemma with finding solid crew continued until I met Michael Thomas. Char and Craig Thomas, my adorable neighbors with whom I shared a driveway, introduced me to their gay nephew. Michael was tall, thin, and handsome. He worked full time in a salon. He was looking for something different and exciting in his life and wanted to give movie-making a try. Sure, movie hair could be defined as different. Yep, let's run with it, because I still have The Boss' "Born to Run" stuck in my head.

I was concerned. Could Michael adapt from working on a customer to pleasing a celeb? Customers' concerns go right out the door when they leave the salon. Celebs will want constant maintenance. Will he commit to crazy long hours? There were also situations where the hairstylist must do his work in the harshest of weather conditions. Could he deal with it? Will he have the patience to rush, rush, rush, wait, wait, wait? Most importantly, how will this affect my friendship with my neighbors, whom I love? If this doesn't work out, and you know it won't, will Char and Craig still agree to plow me out of our driveway when the winter storms hit?

It takes a special someone to fit into this environment. Michael had one big thing going for him. He had "it:" the instant-likeability factor. We started training.

He would need the "it" element immediately. Actors do a search to see how much experience you have. This would be Michael's first entertainment work. He wouldn't have any credits yet. Would he get fired before he even got hired?

After several production meetings, Michael assured me he was ready. I was confident, too. Michael didn't own wheels and it didn't work out to be transported, so we agreed he would drive me home and then pick me up. I had a little sporty convertible that really tripped his trigger. He showed up with a hoodie covering his head, securely tied with a scarf, and big fashion sunglasses. I felt like we were getting ready to take on the Thelma and Louise adventure—probably the one where they were about to hold hands and knowingly drive off the cliff.

Michael started out by altering the typical research on his actors. He studied their interests and then struck up a smooth chat session on a similar book he had read. For some, he relished in-depth discussions theorizing and debating the inner depths of a controversial novel; for others, a light topic conversation on a frolicsome subject matter. He definitely had the right "it."

Not only was Michael well-read, he knew of all the hip places to hang and the adventurous things to do on days off. It was comfortable for him to make appropriate suggestions to the cast. Michael bonded with Hollywood effortlessly.

We also had an easy working relationship. Many times we would read each other's minds and we would share a hidden sarcastic look when a celeb requested the impossible.

"Please don't use water on my hair. I'm super sensitive to water," said the starlet with several cowlicks sticking straight up. Michael and I turned to each other, almost on cue, and his eyes slightly and quickly rolled toward his brows.

Michael believed the finest-looking film department on set would be the one with the best hairstyles. It reminded me of when my daughter Lindsey would fix Taci's hair along with everyone else's on her volleyball team. "The team with the cutest hair will win," Lindsey would always say.

After we got the first round of talent bedazzled and out the door, Michael would insist on putting us in his chair. He would do a little something to complement our wardrobe. Amy would always look forward to this treat. I, however, did not. I would get out of bed and instantly put on a hat. I needed far more help than a touch-up. "Dear God, Trista, did you even comb your hair?" Michael pursed his lips. He was the first to master the pucker-out "duck" lips, before it even had a name.

"Nope, no time." I put on my hat.

Our next project was with Peter Dinklage of *Game of Thrones,* Ryan Kwanten from *True Blood,* and Steve Zahn from *Dallas Buyers Club.* They were a bunch of passionate cats and Michael was the lion king. *Knights of Badassdom* was about live-action role players (LARPs) who mistakenly summoned up a demon from hell and dealt with the consequences. Michael had those boys and the entire community of LARPers summoning gamer-type hairstyles.

We worked a lot of nights on that show. With a call time of 6 p.m., we would have breakfast at 5:30 p.m., lunch at midnight, and dinner at wrap. We shot in a state park in the heat of the summer, and with that comes lots of horrid bugs. We turned off our lights inside the trailer to fend them off, and chuckled at the silliness of working in the dark.

The breaks at the camp dining tent were a real hoot. Lots of tables lined up. You would think we would want to mingle with various crew and sit at other tables. We shared a trailer. We shared our set perch. But no, we inevitably always sat together while eating. Insert "mean girls" image of the high school clique who can't bear to separate. However, it's definitely a good sign when you have crew you choose to be with, even after hours and days of being forced to work together.

Before our next actor, Michael motioned me into his chair. "Holy Jesus, Trista, when was the last time you washed your hair?"

"Umm...can't remember," I muttered.

"You can't be seen like that." He placed my hat back on, wearing latex gloves, and pointed for me to return to the other side of the trailer.

One night the caterers served a bonanza of prime rib and chicken. Michael, Taci, Emily, Amy, and I chatted it up while gnawing on heavy protein. Michael ran and got ice in between our touch-ups on the LARPers. "What's wrong, Michael?" I was worried.

"Meat sweats."

Michael made me laugh.

Often times I would be in the trailer while my crew was on set. To relay information, they would text me. "Are you on your way?" I had a flip phone. Tap, tap, tap the nine key three times, display the Y. Tap and tap the three for E. It was a painful process to type "YES."

"Please bring the Kevin Murphy gel." I would get distracted and not answer. "Did you get the last text?" asked Michael.

Tap W, tap X, tap Y, enter...me of little patience. I opened the door. "Hey Jared, Jared? Tell Michael the gel is on the way," as I handed it to a production assistant running to the set.

Michael texts me. "Do you want me to wait until Steve gets in and do Ryan at the same time?"

I ran to Jared's trailer. "Tell Michael yes, it's a great idea." Another text, another run to Jared, this system made logical sense to me.

What also made sense was the direct correlation between the amount of time that passed without me taking the time to wash my hair, and the distance away from me Michael would perch. In the car ride home, Michael pulled over and stopped the car. He turned to me and said, "We are burning your bed sheets tonight and washing your hair."

Michael moved into a yuppie loft above a hip dance club with his new partner. No one I knew ever moved into a loft. It just made Michael's cool-o-meter go up 100 degrees. He was unusually tired from his move after our early morning call. He called the owner of a fabulous little bistro not too far from his new crib and ordered us a carrot cake. "Bitches, this has been a rough day and we need comfort." When it arrived, we all grabbed a fork and started digging.

No slicing. No serving. Just behaving like carnivores.

Our next actor flew in unexpectedly and interrupted our sugar party. "Sorry, I will come back later." Our actor backed out the door.

"Michael, I think we busted our image."

"What he thinks of us is none-ya," Michael stated matter-of-factly. Noneya business.

When working with Michael, the skies seemed bluer, the grass looked greener, and that was a gray drab winter when we shot *Camilla*. We had a young cast with a few recognizable actors. Carey Elwes of *The Princess Bride* was a dear heart and superbly talented. *Camilla* is a coming-of-age period piece taking place in 1940s New York.

It was during that project that Amy decided to expand her horizons and get her hair license. The elaborate '40s hairstyles of *Camilla* inspired her. She was going to school in between filming days and nights. Amy would continue to do makeup, but also wanted to have hair skills under her belt. Having two reliable talents on my team doing hair: oh happy day.

Toward the end of filming *Camilla*, Michael sat me in my makeup chair. "It kills me to love you, Trista."

He gathered the group and they all held hands in a circle around me. "Welcome to our intervention. Hand over your flip phone. You are no longer allowed to use this. We demand you buy a smartphone."

Michael brought cookies from the same deli that made our carrot cake and I had my own intervention. I licked the cookies and placed them back in the box while Michael watched in horror.

Michael's realism was refreshing and created a magnetism friends yearned for. We were wrapped and waiting for the next gig to come along. This break in the action always causes me anxiety and brings up my abandonment issues, but during our down time, Michael had endless personal invitations. He was excited to attend a wedding and to prep. Michael met Amy for a haircut at her school. She knew

Michael was supportive but probably not thrilled to get a student cut. I can picture the duck lips.

The day after Michael's wedding I received my first call on my new big-girl phone. It was Emily. Hmm, now that Michael and Taci taught me how to text, why call? How do you press, "I want to talk?"

"Are you sitting down?" Emily asked.

"No, why?"

Emily choked out the words. "It's Michael. He passed away."

My heart stopped and the phone dropped.

Taci ran into my office and grabbed my cell phone off the floor.

"What's wrong?" Taci got the details from Emily and then held my hair as I was throwing up.

Evidently, Michael's loft roommate had pills in a pillbox looking similar to his own. He accidentally took something that didn't mix well with the alcohol he had consumed at the wedding.

Several close friends gathered at my home. The recessed lighting in my cathedral ceiling turned off, and then the lights magically went back on. I'm sure this was a sign from Michael. Even when it's darkest there will be light again. Our Thelma and Louise adventure was here. It's the cliff scene. Until death, do us part? It was Memorial Day weekend.

My new phone didn't stop ringing. I received calls from Carey Elwes, along with others all over the world.

Michael's family asked me to give the eulogy. How do I translate all of Michael's goodness and all my fond memories into a speech? How do I make everyone laugh like we did, when all I could do was sob? How do I find the strength even to talk in front of his loved ones?

I asked my friend Nike, an acting teacher and casting director, to help me. I started rehearsing. Nike listened intently as I sped through the funniest of Michael moments. Should I mention the hilarious time he was asked to babysit his girlfriend's small daughters and they went to the public pool? He got worried stares from the passersby when he was waiting for them outside the girls' changing area. Should I try to replicate the strange looks from the protective mother hens? What about the time he was feeling really macho and made every attempt to park my car at basecamp during a snowstorm? All the big burly transpo-guys watched in amusement. When he finally realized the impossible situation, he handed the car keys over to me, as I could visibly see his ego bruising. I rambled and crammed through every Michael anecdote. I was reading from a third-person place so I could deliver the words without breaking down and losing it.

Nike took my stack of story notes and folded them gently and lovingly on my lap. "Trista, this is your experience with Michael. Take your time and everyone will wait for your thoughts. Let your heart do the talking, not your head. Consciously be aware." Nike wisely finished with, "Breathe."

The small funeral home was standing room only with hundreds and hundreds in attendance. Michael's cousin, Luke, a Catholic priest, was presiding over the service. When the introduction music stopped, there was no Luke. I waited for what seemed like an eternity.

I started squirming. "Taci, am I supposed to walk up there now?"

"It's not an award show. You don't get an introduction, Mama."

Amy gave me a squeeze and Cassie gave me an encouraging nod.

Michael's Aunt Char and Uncle Craig were seated in the front row along with his beautiful mom Jo, his dad Steve, and his gorgeous sister Cortney.

As I stood front and center, behind the microphone, I could feel and see the outpouring of grief from Michael's family and friends. My mouth became spit-less and felt like it was stuffed with cotton. I took a deep, slow inhale and as I exhaled, I reminisced about the Michael I knew and loved.

"Michael was a godsend and I was privileged to know him."

I showed a video of pictures the family had gathered and we put it to the music of "Fields of Gold" by Sting. *"Will you stay with me? I've never made promises lightly, some that I've broken. In our days to live we will walk in fields of gold."*

"Michael was a gem who will forever walk on a field of gold," I concluded. Those words still resonate.

After the service, there was a reception at the Char, Craig, and Trista compound.

Beckie and her husband, who do food services for the motion pictures, graciously offered to cater. I texted her when the service was finished to let her know we were heading home. Beckie confirmed she was set up and ready. When I arrived home, there was no Beckie. She had set up at the wrong house. She went to Char and Craig's. Michael's doings, I'm sure; always a waggish spin.

Parking was impossible to find. Cars were lining the street down our hill and out to the main stretch. The Michael stories continued, with hundreds of grievers toasting into the wee hours and through 70 bottles of wine.

Michael would've enjoyed this just like another big shindig when we celebrated Craig's 40 years from Vietnam. We had all dressed up as characters from the *M\*A\*S\*H* show. Craig felt lucky to be alive. He had lost his legs after stepping onto a land mine. His loss never stopped him from doing anything. He was a true hero and inspiration. At Michael's memorial, we wheeled one of the mourners to her designated driver's car in Craig's wheelchair.

A year later, Michael's sister gave birth to Mykul, a beautiful little girl lovingly named after her adored uncle.

When Amy graduated from her training, I gave her Michael's hair shears. We both cried as I was handing over the Olympic torch, forever lighting our shared trailer with his presence.

# Dancer

I had a memorable project in 2005 and I learned several new dance moves.

*Mozart and the Whale* was based on the story of Jerry and Mary Newport, as told in a *Los Angeles Times* article. It's a love story between two savants, "Donald" and "Isabelle." They both had Asperger's, a type of autism. The Asperger's syndrome sabotaged their new, blossoming relationship. The two leads were cast with Josh Hartnett and Radha Mitchell.

Josh's agent called and asked if I could meet Josh and discuss his character. Hartnett hadn't decided if he was going to use me as his makeup and hairstylist; this was a test. I've been through this before. Sometimes Hollywood stars need to know, going in, if our personalities will mesh and whether I will make a good dance partner.

Do they want the likes of me fussing over them 14 hours a day for months? Mr. Agent told me Josh had a bad experience with a former artist. No offense taken, and of all people, I can relate. But secretly, yeah, it feels like I'm back in junior high school at a sock hop and I'm standing against the wall wondering when I will be chosen to dance. Or worse, will I be forgotten?

We met in Studio City at a hair salon. I decided Josh's character shouldn't have a perfectly coiffed hairstyle because "Donald" with Asperger's wouldn't care about his hair. I shared my ideas of having a childlike cut—perhaps make it a little uneven on the forehead, as if "Donald" had experimented with scissors. We had a few laughs and bonded. If Josh only knew how similar "Donald" and Trista were with scissors, I might have been left alone on the dance floor.

Our next tango was to develop the makeup and hairstyles for the remaining characters. A small group of us, including Josh, visited a home where people with Asperger's resided.

A young man swung open the front door before we knocked. "Why are you guys here? To see if we're freaks or something?" That was my first intro to learning the dance moves of those with the syndrome.

One gal was obsessed with getting to her doctor's appointment. She kept repeating the time and date, which wasn't until next Tuesday, but she was afraid she was going to be late.

Another man was rocking back and forth in a stationary chair, hitting the middle of his back each time he swayed. He said it was a soothing reaction, to calm him. I tried it. Strangely, it was. This was definitely a different way to do a chair dance.

I realized each of the housemates displayed different symptoms. It was a range of behaviors that varied in a wide degree with each individual. Mostly, I found challenges in social awkwardness, and as a dancer I often found it necessary to change my choreography.

"Are we going to be famous?" A handsome man was asking me

but looking away. I felt invisible. His one-sided conversation was familiar. *I think I once dated someone with Asperger's.*

I ran into a woman who had a penchant for green lollipops. Perhaps I could use food as makeup. Bingo. This was the kind of stuff that would help my department authenticate the characters in this show. To carry off this habit, we gave one of the characters green lips and then advised the property manager, or props, to have a supply of green apple suckers for her to use during her scenes. There were times when "Donald" could wear his lunch on his face. Mustard is a pretty color.

In *Mozart and the Whale,* the small group of 10 characters had their own separate homes but came together daily in a community center with a psychologist to share their common challenges. This was where Donald met Isabelle. The new girl was an anomaly who became a fascination to Donald.

Isabelle and Donald were highly intelligent and articulate. They had the uncanny focus and ability to express their innermost thoughts verbally. I wanted to be more like that so I tried it.

I announced breaking news to my parents. "I hereby divorce you."

Radha Rani Amber Indigo Anunda Mitchell is an Australian native who started acting in high school. She later moved to Los Angeles, while also having a place in Australia. I adored her accent and her great skin. She took care of herself by eating vegan, and it showed. She had just wrapped *Man on Fire* with Denzell Washington. They'd worked in Mexico City and she shared her stories of fear while filming. Kidnappings were happening feet away from the set. This was the very subject matter with which *Man on Fire* dealt.

While chatting with Radha about the tone of her last movie experience, it was refreshing to have candid, lighthearted fun designing her character, "Isabelle." We added lots of mascara onto her beautiful long lashes. "A girl can never wear too much mascara," Radha said. But with her accent, "mask-cara" gave it new meaning. We gave her hair an extra element of flair by crimping it, and styled her locks with sass and pizzazz just like her character would do, because she played a hairdresser.

All this was unlike the wife and mother character she'd just finished playing with Denzel in Mexico, where she wore her short hair seriously straight and behind her ears. How interesting that someone who isn't skilled with hair (me) would be teaching someone who knows nothing about styling someone else's hair (Radha) in a movie where she played a trained hair stylist (Isabelle). This truly was an irony with curling irons.

The first day of shooting *Mozart and the Whale* was a windy, chilly day at the park along the river. In this first setup, Radha introduced herself to the new Asperger syndrome support group she wanted to join.

She would be questioning her existence, along with sharing her darkest thoughts, and the director asked me to make sure her makeup matched her mood. Translation: he didn't want to be the one to discuss his ideas with her. It felt awkward to ask her to look un-perfect and to un-do all we had just accomplished in the makeup trailer. I felt the music shift in my head to a somber tune. Time again being of the essence, we ran into a public bathroom in the park because the trailer was too far way. This type of situation always makes the actress feel unsettled. Quick, change how you look, but do it before your first scene on the first day and in a strange place, in front of females washing their hands in a public bathroom, or maybe this was exactly the reaction the director was searching. Hmm...keep your actress uncomfortable, especially for this particular scene.

I remembered a different project where I worked with an actress who described this same scenario of being thrown off balance immediately before a vital scene. We were working with director Wayne Wang and this was her second movie with him, my first.

Feihong Yu was flung into the most difficult emotional scene of the entire script just moments after her long travel. Without any warning or preparation, she got off the plane and went straight to set. It was for the movie *Joy Luck Club,* and it was the famous scene where she was drowning her baby in the bathtub.

But I digress—back to Radha and the story at hand. *Mozart and the Whale* was originally slated to have Steven Spielberg direct, but his workload made it impossible. If this was what our replacement director, Petter Naess, was striving for, he was brilliant; catching an actress in a vulnerable state to create an emotionally charged performance gave him what he got.

Radha was agitated as I was removing makeup, smudging her mascara, rushed, and if that weren't enough, we were away from the privacy and well-being of her own trailer. "Isabelle" was up, and she was raw.

"It takes eight minutes for the sun's warmth to travel to the Earth and if the sun were to explode, right now, we will have minutes and then we all die. So isn't that really all the time we are promised?" As Radha delivered an outpouring of emotions on each and every take, the makeup took on an organic realism. No need for me to blow mentholated crystals into Radha's eyes. Her tears danced in unison with her performance. She's one of the few actresses I have ever worked with in my career who could cry on cue. She drew me in, and I cried too. Petter, the director, was extremely pleased. I will never know if he, along with Wayne Wang, manufactured the turmoil.

As filming progressed, I became very aware of the need to keep the makeup and hair expressive and carefree to signify the uniqueness needed to reflect each character. It was a creatively fun way to dance my way through a gig, which brought out the best parts of me.

I gave "Izzy" a lioness eyeliner and wild hair during the day we were shooting at the zoo. That was her nickname given affectionately by Donald. Izzy would be imitating the animals to entertain Donald Duck.

Izzy wore an adorable bunny hat some of the time and in one spontaneous scene, she sported a cute bunny tattoo—on her bare buns. In other shows where there are tattoos, we do a sketch and have sheets made that will transfer onto the skin. However, for "Izzy," we wanted it to be silly and free-spirited so I drew a bunny outline by hand and then filled it in with airbrush.

In one scene, I designed a wig to make her look like 1700s Mozart. With Izzy excitement, we added some pink into the white tight curls.

Donald wore a whale costume. Donald arrived "late, which is ironic, because I started out nine hours and 23 minutes early." I loved the line Josh delivered...it was so "Donald"-ish.

During a special Mozart and the Whale date, Donald told Izzy, "All my life I felt like I was on the sidelines. Uh, watching the parade go by. When you're a whale, you are the parade."

On another shooting day, Izzy cleaned Donald's apartment, so we ponied her hair up. His place was filled with a lifetime of newspapers and knick-knack collections. She removed the clutter and it was unrecognizable.

Donald freaked out, claiming Izzy "took away his life." I can totally relate to Izzy. Clearing space to make room for myself in a man's world, I've had several disastrous relationships with the wrong timing, missteps, and bad beats. Maybe that's why I was single without a dance partner?

Izzy and Donald took a break after that.

I had several makeup assistants, but there were times when I was responsible for several actors on set. I wore this goofy-looking apron with lots of pockets and cubbies to keep everyone's brushes and products separated. Mozart hair, whale costumes, bunny hats, and tats...somehow in the scheme of the project the apron didn't seem as stupid as it could've felt.

I often reflect on Asperger's syndrome and the simple innocence of *Mozart and the Whale*. In remembrance of their characters, I renamed a go-to soft pink lip color I used on Radha. I keep a packet of mustard and my "Izzy" pink inside my kit as a reminder we all have a little Donald and Izzy inside of us. If only I had the courage to express it and dance to a different beat.

# Judge

"Judge not, lest ye be judged." I'm here to say I have judged others; forgive me. At times, my life in the entertainment biz can be a bit whack-o. So when, if ever, is it acceptable to cast judgment on the actions of others? I'll let you be the judge of mine. Please be kind.

I received a phone call, and Jerry told me that a producer friend gave him my number. "I would like to buy a makeover certificate for my wife," Jerry said.

"Oh, I'm so sorry, but I work on location for feature films and television. I don't typically provide that service."

He pleaded with me that his wife was going through a very rough time and he wanted to do something special for her. He caught me in a weak moment, and so I agreed. He wanted to come to my home, but my address is like my age. I never give it out.

Umm...unless you're Tom Hanks—well then yes, you're welcome to stop by, and bring your wife Nancy. I want to meet the woman behind the man and revisit our Boss moment.

We arranged to meet at my friend's hair studio after hours. I use this studio on occasion, for just this type of situation, when I agree to do something really stupid like meeting a stranger. Shoot me.

I heard the front door open and a man entered. I called out, "Can I help you?"

"I'm Jerry. We talked on the phone last week about my wife."

"Oh yes, is she on her way?"

"Well, this is the deal. I'm not married. I need this makeover for myself."

I've done makeup on men, and I have made men look like women for a movie part, but this will be the first time it's been a clandestine arrangement. "I see. Well, what do you have in mind?"

Jerry opened up one of his plastic grocery bags and dumped out a CoverGirl assortment of dated cosmetics. I couldn't really examine the array because his long, dirty, gnarly fingernails stopped me from noticing anything else. In the moment, I judged his unkempt hands. I didn't mean to. I know it's wrong, but I did.

"I'm having a hard time knowing what colors to use. Can you help me?"

Well, as long as he doesn't ask me to give him a manicure, I got this. "Take a seat, Jerry."

"Can you call me Jerianne?

"Sure thing." Can I call him Jeri for short?

I was having flashbacks to when I foraged through Christina Ricci's old Chanel. I guess the brand isn't important, high-end or drugstore, because old is old. I think he picked this stuff up from the thrift store. I proceeded to talk about his products while applying.

After I was finished, he got up and took out a long flowing wig, which had been stashed in another grocery bag. He bent his head, plopped on the hair, and went to the mirror to get a close-up of his made-up face. He pointed his long dirty nails and touched his cheeks and his forehead and smoothed the hair to frame his face. He admired herself.

I instantly felt this was the first time she felt comfortable in her skin. We engaged in a conversation about his nightlife and how excited he was for his friends to see him. It wasn't so much about the makeup or my application, but more about showing an interest in Jerianne's life and supporting his secret. I'd judged him unfairly. This was about acceptance.

Then there are times I'm surely judged, or should have been, like the time Amy and I were driving home in a monster snowstorm. When we reached her neighborhood, the snow was above my bumper. I slowed down and insisted she jump out of my moving rig so I wouldn't get stuck. Good God, I could've killed my BFF, but she seriously has yet to judge me about anything.

However, when I was filming with Jared Harris, he had every reason to judge me. Before his close-up, the cameraman told me Jared had a nose hair that was visible. Using small medical scissors with rounded edges is always my go-to and first line of attack. However, this particular time I used tweezers to remedy the snarly nose hair. I grabbed onto the little sucker and pulled. Jared winced and yelped—after all, it did make him bleed, and not just a little. I mean, this was a gusher, straight from a gory horror flick. Pretty sure Jared didn't trust me after that incident and he had every reason to cast judgment.

I have occasionally judged the producers who find dates—not as in the date we commence in filming, but as in of-the-opposite-sex dates—for their leading men while we film on locations away from home.

One day after work I stopped off to meet a girlfriend for a drink.

I glanced over to an adjoining private lounge area and there was Sergio, the top-credited star of our show, at the bar surrounded by six gorgeous women, along with the producer. Sergio owns a cologne brand and the smell must be intoxicating, because he was a woman magnet.

The following week his beautiful wife arrived and camped out in his personal trailer during the remainder of the project. It's as if she caught a whiff of his behaviors from the week prior.

I tip my hat to the successful Hollywood marriages, but I have seen a lot of train wrecks, and this type of behavior sadly causes one to judge.

Case in point: I worked with an actor I filmed with often and who'd always treated me with the utmost respect. However, he was a different man during his time off. He had a tendency to drink excessively while dancing all night, hitting on and subsequently sleeping with multitudes of women.

I accidentally saw a text message between one of my makeup assistants and this same actor. I shot Brandi a harsh look of disdain.

"Don't worry, Trista. He told me he and his wife have an arrangement," Brandi explained.

"What kind of 'arrangement?'" I couldn't imagine any logical excuse.

"It's an open marriage."

"What does that mean? Do he and his wife agree it's a two-way street or does he have an unmarked one-way?" Brandi shrugged at my comment.

Several years later he and his wife divorced. Their open marriage became a dead end.

I always judge directors who say, "Daphne, do you think you should have that dessert? You have the lingerie scene tomorrow." Body-shaming is never acceptable. I say plea justifiably guilty.

While filming with Carmen Electra, we had a very short scene, which normally would take a few hours to wrap up. However, she was exiting from a luxurious bubble bath. Those male directors took all day, shame on them.

Several years ago I was in Vegas celebrating my girlfriend's birthday. We were having dinner and a group of guys at the adjacent table suggested we combine our parties because his friend was also having a birthday. The attractive honoree wore a baseball cap.

"Hi, I'm Leonardo."

"Yeah, you are." I melted.

We spent the evening celebrating with Leonardo DiCaprio, a kind and genuine man. The following week there were published rumors about the event. Only a fraction of the story was true. I've been a witness to celebrity gossip before. Hmm...am I judging the judgers?

When I worked with Michael Gladis, he auditioned with his infamous *Mad Men* beard for a role in my next movie project. After he was cast, he shaved his beard without asking. When Gladis arrived to shoot, he had no beard.

The directors and producers were shocked.

I couldn't help but critically judge Gladis for not thinking before he shaved his exquisite beard. Each and every day I spent hours upon hours laying down strands upon strands of hair to recreate what God had naturally provided for him before he shaved. We bonded over our mutual frustrations and had a few laughs.

Something I can't help but judge is how people treat others while they're being served. You can gather a lot of pertinent information on a first date by how your companion interacts with the waitress. I judge actors the same way.

On day one of our new movie, the production assistant was making his rounds, visiting each occupied chair in my trailer and gathering breakfast orders from the actors, none of whom I had worked with in the past. I observed how the celebrities interacted and requested their breakfast orders. It reminds me of when I'm playing poker and I'm watching the other players to gather valuable intel that, in turn, helps me win the game.

"Dry toast and egg whites, please. Thank you, Jillian," said the actress to the production assistant. Yes, I judged she would be lovely to work with.

"Just coffee, black," said my leading actor with a smile. More yes, please, he will be just as lovely.

"I need you to listen to me," said Charles, my other lead actor. "I want my eggs over easy, and if they come back overcooked I will send them back. I want stir-fry veggies, with caramelized onions and no green peppers. Do not use butter, only steam. Bring it to me hot. I don't want to reheat it. And for Christ's sake, don't forget the condiments."

I took his ordering as a signal. Stop the world, Charles needed to get off.

Personal phone conversations can also lead to all sorts of reasons to judge. While working with Flint, I heard him use his time in my chair to talk to his baby's mama. He always used the ever-so-popular privacy feature on his cell phone, the speaker.

"Karen, I told you I don't want Sierra this weekend."

"Flint, it's in the parenting plan. I—"

Karen was interrupted.

"Listen to me, you little bitch, my life doesn't revolve around the court system. I tell you what works. You got it?" yelled Flint.

If past behavior is the best indication of future behavior, I felt sorry for anyone in Flint's life. Sins of the father and wounds of the womb, we are all wrapped individually and perhaps pre-wired, but it didn't stop me from wondering at the degree of wrongfulness.

Flint and Charles are both actors I'm sure every jury, following proper deliberation, would unanimously agree on—and render a verdict of guilty. Let's give them a life sentence of living together on a separate planet from the rest of us.

On my next project, I was meeting with the director, Joan, during pre-production and she wanted to include me on a phone conversation she was about to have with our lead actor, Phil. She didn't agree with Phil on his interpretation of his character and she shared some of her concerns with me.

"Trista, in scene 112, don't you agree he should look haggard, and then when we see him again in 115, he looks ill?" She dialed up his number.

"Good morning, Phil, I have Trista here. Let's discuss makeup. Trista, go ahead. Tell Phil your thoughts."

I was caught off guard. Yes, I had my script notes, but I'd never met Phil and I wasn't prepared to be Joan's messenger.

Phil knew he had power over Joan and judged her as inept. He used a ladder on set to look down on her as she directed. Each day when Phil entered the makeup trailer, he would hit his head on the living room overhead cupboards.

To help him out, Amy hung colored flags we hoped would act as a reminder not to get close. It worked the first few days. However, eventually the predictable occurred: Phil, with his head in the clouds, ignored the warning flags, and thumped his head on the cupboard. Despite ripping down the streamers, and his incessant cursing and huffing, karma prevailed and it was a bitch.

I judged a Hollywood prima donna who invited me to an exclusive party and I was so honored. That is, until I realized I was there so I could touch up her makeup in the women's lounge. I believe this falls under bait-and-switch or at least misleading a not-so-public servant.

I recall a time when Cassie, my massage therapist, entered her treatment room to find my male thespian standing buck naked.

He asked her for more than a massage, with a happier ending. Isn't that indecent exposure, as it certainly caused alarm and affront?

For the privacy of people who brave the life under the bright lights, I rarely invite my friends to the makeup trailer. However, I had a friend who picked me up at the end of my day for a glass of wine.

Just as Trebor opened the door, Joey Pantoliano, an Emmy winning

Italian-American character actor, was taking off his pants. Trebor found himself in one of those defining moments: do his eyes deceive him? Should he come in or excuse himself as he backs out and shuts the door? Regardless, at that moment, Trebor pre-judged us both by making assumptions or assuming facts not presented into evidence. Little did he know, Joey wanted me to duplicate a tattoo he had on his leg and place it on his arm. "Pants," his nickname way before this incident, authored *Who's Sorry Now,* a memoir. How profound.

The most bizarre requests for makeup and hair applications are on animals, usually dogs, but you should never rule out my work with seals, chickens, bunnies, pigs, elephants, giraffes, goats, cats, and birds. Zookeeper I'm not; judged, yes.

In one dumb-criminal flick, the thieves robbed a jewelry store and actually hid diamonds inside their dog. Yep, I had to apply special-effect stitches on her underbelly. Attempting to get the poor canine victim to lie on her back required more than just the two hands of one makeup artist. The whole thing was beyond entertaining to all who witnessed the calamity.

Recently, I added dozens of hair extensions and bows to "Blondie." I think every horse should have a long, flowing, beachy wave mane. Right?

On another project, I worked with several dogs at the same time. They all shared the same role in the film, appearing as if they were just one dog, like when the Olsen twins shared the same part on *Full House.* Tom the dog was better at sitting, Pete was a pro at barking on command, and Lady was proficient at playing catch. The hero dog had different color markings so I painted similar marks on all of them to make them look the same. I chased dog tails on a merry-go-round and learned new tricks.

Let me assure you that the makeup I used was non-toxic. I'm curious when I read disclaimers on skincare products that say they are not animal-tested. Hmm...please rest assured, PETA. It's good enough for my most sensitive-skinned clients.

My biggest difficulty was holding them still. If only we could've taken a page out of Darcy's playbook. Remember, she was the actress who preferred I did her makeup while she slept. Dogs had no special requests, just a treat at the end of the session. Perhaps my superstars could take a page from the doggie playbook?

So okay, I'm dog-challenged. The whole world can judge me, and Taci would totally agree. She would be driving home from work to find her dogs running away from the house with the leashes dangling behind them. Actually, her dogs are small ponies: a Great Dane mix and a black lab. I knew my version of walking the dogs was distinctive: they run loose and I walk back to the house and wait for their return.

Taci was appalled, but I tried to make it up to her. When she came in the house, I bent down over the ponies and said, "Oh, you're such good doggies." Taci was pleased with my obvious affection.

She asked me to look at something irritating her face. I reached to examine her and she paused.

"Don't you want to wash your hands after petting the dogs?" After all, she's a germ-phobia princess just like myself. The antibacterial cleanser doesn't fall far from the tree.

"Oh, I didn't touch them!"

"What? You fake-loved my dogs!"

Caught. Red-handed.

Sometimes I judge an entire profession.

It was Shane McMann's first time running for Congress and I was hired for his commercials and debates. He had a small group of campaign assistants, managers, and volunteers who led the way behind the scenes.

"Our top priority is his perceived visual image," Vicky the campaign manager exclaimed. I wondered if Vicky had taken a visual of her own image in the mirror? Being a trained observer of judging sorts, I could see the remnants of her orange lipstick, which had jumped right off her lips and was now fully present on her teeth. Adding insult to injury, her clothes were four sizes too small, producing gaps between each of the buttons of her stretched blouse. The files she was holding had no organizational theme whatsoever.

The campaign assistant, Penn, covered his phone and shouted, "Vicky, what is the status on those mailers we sent to the printers?"

Vicky ruffled through her papers, conspicuously leaving a trail of files as she searched and moved from room to room.

"Trista, Shane's first shot will be meeting with the agriculture committee. His wardrobe is in the back of my car." She tossed me the car keys. "We have 20 minutes."

I think it meant, "On your mark, get set, go!" Damn, I didn't know I was doing wardrobe too. I ran out to her car and despite those keen observation skills I mentioned, I failed to see anything resembling "wardrobe" on hangers. Instead, I was forced to rummage through what appeared to be dirty laundry. I tossed aside a grease-soaked fast food bag and somehow scored a shirt, tie, and pants from the bottom of her floorboard. The shirt was saturated with stains and his pants needed hemming.

As I scrambled inside with my transient-person mess in hand, Vicky hollered, "He needs to be polished and professional."

Am I being punked? Penn cradled his phone to his ear and handed Vicky a memo. "This outlines the Farm Bureau and the PAC."

As Shane sauntered in, Vicky pushed him toward me. "Great timing, I will get you up to speed while Trista gets you ready."

"All this fuss, Vicky, is this important?" Shane squirmed.

Meaning—to said trained observer—make him feel comfortable because he clearly isn't. "Mr. McMann, I'm Trista." I shook his hand and generated warm thoughts to hopefully translate into "I care about you." I felt his tenseness and uneasiness.

"So where do you want me?"

"Sit right here, Mr. McMann," I said as I pointed him to the only, and I mean only, tabled area I could see that had one ounce of clear space. "I'll just do a little camera prep. It will be painless, I promise," which prompted a short sigh of annoyance. "Is it okay if we take these off for a moment?" As I reached for his glasses, I sensed his obvious irritation. Please don't be bothered. I'm not undressing you. I gingerly propped his glasses on a tissue. "Would you like a bottle of water?" That's always a safe comforting token of consolation.

Penn entered and pushed his phone into the face of Shane. "It's Barnes, he needs to talk to you about tonight's fundraiser." Shane took the phone and exited the room.

Okay. That gave me time to address his "wardrobe." I attacked the stain with my reliable spot-treater; blow-dried, steamed, and taped the hem just in time for Shane's re-entrance.

"Mr. McMann, I will have you change into your wardrobe before continuing." He unwittingly uttered a sigh of sheer exasperation.

While he changed, I pondered the short list of conversation topics safe to explore with a politician. Last week I was a Democrat, yet today I'm a Republican. I'm a chameleon when asked to state my party allegiance. Do as the Romans do, but politics are off limits for me. How's the weather? Lame. How are you today? Lamer. "Do you have children, Mr. McMann?"

"Two boys. Carson is serving in the Air Force..."

He talked about his two biggest achievements, which consumed him long enough to divert his attention from my work. Makeup completed, neck to ears. I have always been fixated on David Letterman's ears because they were always a different color than his face and neck due to the makeup. He's the funniest man in the world and that's what I notice? I'm pathetic.

"...and Cameron is graduating from high school. He..."

I'm distracted due to Shane's strange haircut. It's not farfetched to assume he was impatient and likely perturbed during his last appointment, leaving before the stylist could finish. She probably didn't ask the golden question about his sons. I will need to work in some maximum-strength highly potent product quickly before he jumped out of this chair and ran for the hills.

Vicky rushed in. "Shane, let's get one of the agricultural committee members interested in being a candidate on the board of trustees. Maybe Lang or Landon?"

Shane hesitated. "Okay, I will dangle the question and see who bites."

Vicky pushed on. "If they ask you about your interests, talk about your grassroots efforts."

Holy guacamole, the mere mention of "grassroots" reminded me to double-check the status of the stain removal on his shirt.

Shane put on his glasses while he and Vicky discussed the notes on the shot list (a detailed list of where the camera will be shooting). I taped his tie to his shirt so it wouldn't move. Ties always need to be aligned perfectly straight. Nothing worse than a crooked tie; yet another judging fixation of mine: ties, ears, and politicians.

He shook the committee member's hands. The camera panned to him and Shane opened with, "I want to represent Warshington." He didn't just pronounce Washington with the letter r, did he? Wow. Will the fact he wore glasses make him appear smarter? Will the two cancel each other out? Am I judging? You betcha.

I recalled a political debate I was part of way back when. Terry Hanson, a want-to-be senator was trying to oust a popular deep-seated Washington insider. "What made you want to run for Congress, Mr. Hanson?" Blah-blah-blah.

"Trista, what are your thoughts on Initiative 822?" he eventually asked.

"Mr. Hanson, what are your family plans for Thanksgiving?" I always had a transitional question on hand.

"We are going snowmobiling up at our cabin." Operation Conversation-diversion underway. Terry turned his attention again to politics, talking about why he wanted to get involved. He felt the need to serve after his long career in law. One of his political promises was to serve just one term. He was adamant, and ranted in his campaign speeches he would never be a "career politician."

Every two years I get busy with political commercials, appearances, and debates. It can get tricky billing the politicians. Terry set up a corporation to handle the business of his campaign.

Then he closed the very same corporation when the election was over. I had a nightmare: my job was being an accountant in a hospital and I asked dying patients to prepay their bill. Send the invoice before the election. Terry for Senator, LLC becomes invalid in December. Fast-forward 12 years and he was still in office. I don't know. Is it technically a career? Judges say yes.

A group of advocates took a trip to the other side of the state to show their support for the film industry before the House Ways and Means Committee meeting. We packed the Capitol courtroom to promote a state movie initiative. We had compiled oodles of documents showing how filming in our state boosted the many areas of our overall economy, ranging from a minimum wage worker at a fast food restaurant, or corporate earnings and free advertisement of hotel chains, to increased sales for lodging resulting in tax revenues for local governments.

We had graphs and information proving the business and occupation tax dollars alone would pay for the incentive plan we submitted. I was ready to answer any question that happened to be thrown my way. I had studied the petition and was ready and able to sound intelligent and knowledgeable, especially since I could pronounce "Washington." I sat in the front row purely by accident because I really am a behind-the-scenes, off-camera type of gal who prefers being secreted in the back corner. To my dismay, our representative walked straight up to me. I held out my hand and introduced myself. "Mr. Boone, I'm Trista, District 5."

"Trista, welcome. I'm curious: of all the movies you have filmed, what's your favorite?"

My mouth surely dropped. I'm ready to spiel facts and figures as to why the incentives will financially benefit our state, and you ask me a trivial, meaningless question I would expect from my seven-year-old dotdot (granddaughter). Is that all you've got?

"Ahh..."

"Was it the one with Antonio Banderas?" he asked.

"Um, well..."

The House Ways and Means leader pounded his gavel. "We are back in session." I slumped back onto the bench, defeated and demoralized.

Later, a smaller group went to Mr. Boone's office to speak to him directly. There were piles upon piles of folders on every inch of his office desk, floor space, and the desks of his assistants; it was all covered in mountains of paperwork. That was a familiar sight as I momentarily flashed back to Shane, Vicky, and Penn. Boone didn't show up for our scheduled meeting, so I had time to judge—I mean wonder—how any one person could possibly know the facts, details, pros, and cons of every file stacked in his office and have the intellect to decide how to best represent all constituents in a responsible manner.

It was then that I knew the answer to his nonsensical "favorite movie" question. I wished I had answered, "Sir, they were all my favorites because they employed me, and a crew of lighting, sound, electricians, construction workers, location experts, wardrobe, transportation, caterers, scenic artists, directors, producers, and writers, as well as provided me with additional revenues for all the businesses in the community. I also have to work every day for health insurance, unlike you."

I found political debates always entertaining, especially when I studied up on the issues. It also helped when I did makeup on the very top of the chain. I felt like I had the insider track on truth. I was doing makeup on a commander of an Air Force base. During his on-camera interview, he addressed the subject of pilots flying inside war zones and the precision required to land within compounds (confined areas) with pinpoint accuracy. Our local newspaper reported a controversy over a large commercial complex being approved for construction, due to its close proximity to our local Air Force base. The commander said his pilots found that notion insulting to their prodigious talents and found no conflict with their clearly defined airspace.

The next day I was doing last looks on a political debate and the two candidates were arguing the very same topic. Despite neither one knowing the real truth of this matter, both bantered back and forth about nothingness, as long as it sounded plausible...and I judged their knowledge.

Back to Shane McMann and his campaign. After months of mispronouncing "Warshington" in his stained clothing, Shane won the election. I ran into him at a town hall forum months after he started his first term in office and, as you can imagine, I noticed his tie was crooked. I know it's not a parallel indicator of his character, but more importantly, do we or do we not judge others when we cast our ballot? Do we have all the facts; have we asked all the right questions? Are we making a decision and formulating a judgment without ample information? Is this the time and place to judge? You be the judge.

I wrapped on the Hudson River, where I met Lady Liberty, and I was on my way to my next shooting location in Brooklyn. It was my first time taking the subway. I was alone on my section of the train when four black teens blocked the two side entrances. I couldn't help but react suspiciously when one of the boys reached his hand toward the bottom of his pant leg. I was surprised when he turned on the boom box and they entertained me with hip-hop dance moves. I liked the subway; no positioning for power over an airplane's middle armrest. When I emerged from the station, I entered a black neighborhood. I was immediately taunted by a group of girls chanting, "White chick, go home." If I click my heels together will I wake up in Kansas? A black man, who was six-feet forever and wearing a t-shirt that read, "You're nobody 'til somebody kills you," quickly approached me. I would let him have both armrests on the plane. Hell, he can have my seat too. He grabbed my rolling kit and with the biggest genuine smile he said, "Where are you heading? Here, let me help you." I gave Jamal the address as he escorted me. Jamal explained I was in one of the highest-crime neighborhoods in America, Bed-Stuy. "There was a murder yesterday, a few blocks over. Listen!" As if on cue, I heard a police siren and within seconds an ambulance siren. "Today you will hear a lot of those, but notice the cadence." Jamal expounded on how the emergency responders changed the rhythm of their sirens with every call because the citizens were immune to the sounds.

Jamal hung around and assessed the filming process. I'm sure we judged each other's unfamiliar worlds, but in the end, "You're nobody 'til you can look past judgments."

# Babysitter

One of my first actors in this business was Jack Scalia, not a well-known actor. I remembered him in lots of small television roles and the popular soap opera *All My Children*. Our first play date in the makeup trailer centered on a scar I was to create. The movie back-story for Jack's character included his entanglement at sea with a wild, fierce, gargantuan turtle that gouged his face. Turtles only have a role in G-rated, low-budget flicks, like that one. I suggested to Jack it would be fun if I removed some of his eyebrow and ran the scar down through the missing hair and etched down past his eye. This didn't sound appealing to him, and how would he have the patience to sit in my chair any longer than deemed necessary? Oh great, a fidgety playmate who doesn't want to play by my rules. As a babysitter, the use of distractions and persuasion is vital. I went over to my music playlist and started jamming on some '70s Van Morrison. "Moondance" pacified Jack into submission. Our daily routine consisted of applying the scar while listening to Van the Man. My playground was in harmony. I used a super-fast scar-building material. It maintained extremely well while we filmed and I never had to make adjustments during last looks.

Weeks into the schedule, while waiting for a camera set-up, Jack Scalia played hide and seek and slipped away to his trailer with his girlfriend. Their rough-housing rearranged the placement of what should've been a rock-solid scar. When he returned to set and I viewed the damages, I was previewing the comments on those movie message boards about one scene, and they give it the evisceration: *The Scar That Moved.* So when they called last looks on Jack, I couldn't ignore it. On bigger budget movies, the talent is sent to the makeup trailer after any actor breaks for my inspection and touch-ups, but we were working on a lower-than-dime-store chintzy film.

Hello, this is about a turtle.

The critic's title of *The Scar That Moved* was ringing in my ears way louder than the directors' scoffing and looking at their watches. Actually, who will watch this cheesy movie? Will children watch with their nannies? Should I even care? Yes, I care. As we listened to Van Morrison's "Comfortably Numb," one of Jack's favorites, I removed the remnants and reapplied the scar liquid while the camera department rolled their eyes to the back of their heads instead of rolling the camera. I had to keep tabs on Jack and his girlfriend for any extracurricular activities to keep the scar in place. Babysitting can be exhausting.

To this day, I think of turtles and child's play when I hear the music of the Northern Irish singer-songwriter Van Morrison.

I recall this other movie when I did an elaborate, three-hour, severed arm special effect. After I finished hacking the actor's arm, the director fondly approved of my masterpiece of blood, painting, and wax molding. While the actor waited for his call to set, he played his guitar next to a wood stove in the base camp cabin. Yep, you know what comes next. He ignored the heat and his severed forearm gash slid into a pool of flesh to his wrist. He felt awful when he finally noticed the destruction.

Esther Elise, one of the best A.D.s in the industry, watched me recreate the messed-up special effects makeup on the set while we were both under serious time deadlines. I knew it would never look the same as the original because I was rushed and I wasn't in my trailer, but I felt crushed in disappointing the director. As a babysitter, I learned never to allow my child, I mean actor, near fire.

I've had talent decide to put on more of their own mascara in the privacy of their trailer, only to come to set with a face trail of flaky black-dotted dried fiasco. As a babysitter I must never allow actors to be unattended.

However, this was not true with late great Garry Marshall; he was in and out of my makeup chair within seconds. "Let's keep it real," Garry said. I never had to attend to him.

Oh, and there was this unforgettable failure, while filming with Lainie Kazan on *Oy Vey, My Son is Gay*. Lainie is famous for her role in *My Big Fat Greek Wedding*. We created an appliance to duplicate the two-finger facelift with two thin stretch cords. Young women will never be able to relate to this. Those mini bungees were tightened with bobby pins attached to her hair at the back of her head and then hidden under her wig. This trick worked fantastically, and no one knew why she looked so much younger after she finished in the makeup chair. Imagine my shock when my last looks revealed a pin had slipped out of place. My toy was broken and affected only the camera-left side of her face. She appeared to have had a stroke, because one side of her face drooped. Good thing this babysitter didn't have to call 9-1-1. The emergency was negated. Oh, the hustle to discreetly fix Humpty Dumpy together again. Oy!

There have been numerous projects where I worked with children, and sometimes I babysit not the child but the parent.

Savi arrived with her mom, Peggy, and my job was to make sure Savi didn't have gnarls in her hair and food on her face. Savi was six years old and she showed up wearing more makeup than her mother would on a dress-to-the-nines glamour night out in Vegas.

As I washed Savi's face to remove all the makeup—because the scene took place in a classroom, not in a clown school—Peggy gloated on the next gig her daughter was cast in. I'm sure Savi lived in Hollywood before she left Peggy's womb.

While I brushed out Savi's prom hair up-do, Peggy rehearsed Savi's lines, which she knew verbatim. I wondered if Peggy would've given up her own left leg to be a star.

When we arrived to the set, my primary function with this group of children was to make sure they didn't appear as if they'd rubbed a balloon on their heads. Kids are active and their hair can change in a flash, so I planned to fix it right before the camera rolled.

I was ready with my supply of hair goop nested on my wrist for quick access when I noticed Peggy standing next to Savi in front of the camera, applying lip-gloss to her starlet daughter.

When last looks was up, Peggy took it as her prompt to do final touches on Savi's hair. She whipped out her tools and proceeded.

As I watched the monitor during the first take, Peggy pushed her way to the front. There was confusion as to why Peggy was in an area designated for crew members only, so I said, "Let me introduce you to my new makeup assistant. Her name is Stage Mom, and her daughter pays the mortgage."

On another occasion it wasn't small children with parents playing, but grown men. The pyro guy took most of the morning setting up the explosive stunt. The cameras were set up at numerous exterior locations so the editors could choose which angle worked best. One window in the abandoned building was to blow out, imitating a blast from a weapon. I wasn't prepared for the results of what was to be a simple glass mess down below onto the adjacent parking lot. Not just one window was affected, but every window on every floor propelled glass. The shockwaves could be felt from miles away and the whole city heard the explosion.

The director and producer simultaneously were sickened and brought out their phones. I, on the other hand, started cheering along with the crowd. That was my first experience with stunts. You just never know what's going to happen, and sometimes it goes terribly wrong. What do I want to be when I grow up? Sign me up for babysitting stunts and my next gig was just that.

We waited for the train before I heard, "Action." Right before the train hits the mark, the stunt double raced his car across the tracks, missing the train by a nano-second, ditching the car, pursuing the chase. This was life or death and I loved the adrenaline rush, but why was I really there? Pinch me—I needed a babysitter to keep my inner child in check.

They hoped to get the train chase in one shot. The next train wasn't due for 30 minutes. There were numerous cameras mounted strategically on both cars and they were carefully aimed not to expose the stunt men's faces, otherwise the audience would know they'd replaced the actors. I used wigs on the stunt men to match the color and style of the actors' hair. Is this why I have a job? To babysit a wig? Please wig, fall off.

Then there were times when I made mannequins look like the actor. This would happen, for example, if they needed to have a knife stuck in their eye or be buried in the dirt inside a body bag. I remember such a scene in the bottom of a rock quarry. It was winter and the middle of the night.

My department wore Carhartt jackets and masks, and we sported flashlights on our foreheads. It was a dreary, ominous scene burying a dead body, a.k.a. mannequin. To brighten the mood, we painted kitty cat whiskers on our protective nose wear. We were there to babysit the painted mustache on the dummy and make sure the gallons of blood poured on the body didn't cover up our work.

That was not as exhilarating as the time I was appointed to work with Johnny Martin, an award winning stunt director with boyish good looks, Elvis hair, and a damn impressive résumé, including credits like *The Italian Job,* along with a few hundred more.

He also hired his stunt buddy, Michael Papajohn or Pop, an Alabama native with a Greek heritage, widely known as the car-jacker in *Spider-Man* whose actions ultimately lead Peter Parker to become Spider-Man.

Pop also played Kevin Costner's nemesis in *For Love of the Game.* I'm in love with the game of stunts.

Johnny and Pop met while working together on *Titanic.* They were drowning together in and out of the boat for months while directed by James Cameron.

Johnny was setting up a stunt where a metal pole would pierce through the front windshield, impaling Pop while his character was on a hot car pursuit. Johnny conducted endless dry rehearsals to ensure Pop's safety for this one-and-done take. I saw a note on Pop's script. It said NAR.

As I was doing last looks, because this babysitter was there to keep his handsome mug from looking sweaty during this intense stunt, I asked Pop, "What does NAR stand for?"

Before Pop answered, I heard Johnny call out, "Action."

"No. Acting. Required," said Pop.

Pop has died more times on screen than any other actor in Holly-wood. Another day and another scene was up in which Pop voluntari-ly placed himself in imminent danger. In this movie he was thrown up against walls and continuously hit by the good guys. I guess that would make him the bad guy. I applied a styptic to stop his bleeding, before adding fake blood...something ironic about that.

The following evening, he severely bruised his hip while doing a stunt, and it required him to visit the emergency room. It was impossible to keep him out of harm's way; I think my days as a babysitter were numbered.

Pop and I became friends, and after the production wrapped I used my babysitting allowance to join Pop in Hawaii. We continued our stunt adventures, charting a yacht for deep-sea fishing. How appropriate it didn't go without incident. We caught, and I only use the word "we" because I kissed the enormous lure, a 341-pound blue marlin. The marlin had to be worn out before surrendering, so reeling her in took hours. When Pop got her in closer, the marlin had a childish tantrum and lashed out with a vengeance, puncturing the boat. My gig as a babysitter went out with a bang when the captain had no choice but to shoot her.

# Cheerleader

As a makeup artist, I have learned to do mental cheerleading flips and cartwheels in mid-air. Statistics show cheerleading carries the highest rate of catastrophic injury in sports.

"Can you take away these wrinkles?" Vivianne asked as she pursed her lips and brought her hand mirror closer to her eyes.

"Of course, my dearie," I replied. That is my number one request, but in this circumstance I will not give my standard shtick of "I can minimize the appearance" which is what every wrinkle cream bottle in the universe states, but I wear kid gloves when I'm with Vivianne. I used my trio of wrinkle minimizers and layered it on twice.

"It doesn't appear to be working, Trista." Vivianne inspects with her magnifying mirror. "Perhaps I should have stayed in bed today?"

"Oh, sweetie, it takes a few minutes for my close-up cocktail to do the trick." I assured her, as she laughed with her mouth closed.

"Well, I never roll out of bed for less than 20K; I shouldn't have made an exception."

Oh barf. Gag me now.

"What do you think of these earrings? Dahling, I'm just not sure. Is it the shape or the color or what?" she said very slowly.

"Well, in this scene you have a lot of dialogue, right? Do you think, and I'm just wondering, is there a distraction from the clunky swinging of the earrings?" I carefully suggest.

"Mmm, yes. I will talk to wardrobe. Trista, I'm not sure if my bangs are too long?"

"Oh let's snap a photo. A picture never lies."

I showed her my phone screen with the results. I didn't dare say they are the perfect length. She was one of those personality types that always wanted the opposite. You know those people? When you say black, they say white.

"Trista, maybe I should have the bangs pushed back into my hair?"

"Yes, let's try it." I was treading water.

She looked into the mirror. "We just aged 10 years, Trista."

We didn't age. You aged. If I had a dimmer switch on my vanity lights, I would use it. Soft lighting always turns back years. "Today, I think the bangs are youthful. Shall we keep them?" I asked while tiptoeing. What else can I do? You have bangs or you don't.

"Trista, are my eyebrows the right shape? Should we add more definition?"

We had redefined them six times and I used three different colors for perfection. Pretty sure if we added any more product, it would become a uni-brow. "Yes definitely, let me touch them up, let's add a skosh of deeper color right here at the top of the arch...Yes, that's it. Do you like?"

"The left brow doesn't look *exactly* like the right one," Vivianne said.

"They are sisters, sweetie, not twins," I said.

"Oh and darling, I'm not sure about my neck, it appears to look, um, maybe, oh I don't know."

Vivianne studied her cleavage as I powdered and blended and used a slightly darker color under her jaw to contour and also between her exposed breasts to show a plunging décolletage. I did this exact same thing an hour ago, so I felt like a cheerleader doing back flips, with the need for protective equipment. I repeated the steps using a smidge of product.

"Trista, I think I need a half of a lash on the outer third of this other lash and..."

Give me a D!

Give me an I!

Give me a V!

Give me an A!

What's that spell?

This cheerleader was in the midst of an ultimate exercise of vocal restraint. When I see those commercials where they have the subtitle, "Real people, not actors," I have to marvel. Aren't actors real people? Let me answer for you: yes. Vivianne? No.

"Dahling, when you look from this angle here, do my ears need cleaning? Is there dry skin you can address?" Vivianne held her mirror at an impossible angle to the side.

Would now be a good time to remind Miss Thing this interview was inside?

That there will be no blowing air like Marilyn Monroe over the grate of the New York sidewalk?

"No one is going to see your ears!" Oh no, did I just say that out loud?

Our father who art in heaven, hallowed be thy name, thy kingdom come...

"Oh honey, let me check. Yes, they look perfect." I've got spirit, yes I do. I've got spirit, how about you?

"What about behind my ears?" Vivianne asked.

I'm no longer tiptoeing. I'm walking on a bed of glass shards in my bare feet. See how dangerous cheerleading can be?

"Trista, I do think my ears are sticking out, can you...?"

"I'm on it." I scrounged through my medicinal pouch and grabbed some medical glue to lay down the ears. Hello, retirement, are you calling my name?

After hours and hours of touch-ups, Vivianne was ready to check in with wardrobe, using a secret passage because she couldn't be seen by anyone. She also had strict rules that no one ever have eye contact with her while she was on set. Or ever. And she wanted minimal crew around her, if crew needed to come to set to do their job they had to wait in the wings until she left.

I traveled to set un-secretly to re-check her makeup, knowing that if something was amiss I had to travel back to her dressing room to address. She was a stunningly beautiful woman before I even touched her, but there was no such thing as my reality, just her perception.

Divas require a finesse that surpasses the needs of all other species known to mankind. She not only needed my talents as an artist, but also needed my cheers to be on top of her game, even if most of them were only heard in my own head.

Vivianne reminded me of my mother—the queen of ice.

On my mother's deathbed I racked my brain to remember a hug, a cheer of encouragement, even a connection. Nothing, but she taught me how to be a damn good mother to my daughters. I raised them the total opposite way.

Not all cheering is dramatic like it was with Vivianne. Sometimes cheerleading can be effortless.

The production company arrived at the farm of the Garrison family and we were warmly greeted with treats and juices. Mac Garrison's grandparents homesteaded this sprawling cattle ranch, where he also raised his family. He was in his late 60s and had Parkinson's disease. We were filming a documentary about a surgery

Mac had six months prior to treat his symptoms of Parkinson's.

The Garrisons had never experienced behind the scenes or being in front of the camera, so they were new to the entire process. They didn't know we were going to completely rearrange their entire house, turn off all their phones, isolate their pets, borrow shit, and with any luck, not scrape any paint off the walls or doors while we hauled in our gear.

I laid down my towel on their kitchen table facing a big picture window and set up my standard rolling bag of wares while introducing myself.

"Wow, I've never seen so much hair product and powder," said Dorothy, the wife. "Mac, look at all this stuff Trista needs to put on you to make you pretty."

"I'm going to give you red lips and blue eye shadow Mac, are you up for it?" As I applied makeup on Mac, his eyes got big and Dorothy and I chuckled while the family took pictures of us.

"If you don't behave, Mac, I've got extortion photos to embarrass you." His wife raised her phone with the stored evidence.

The family was giddy with the newness of the experience. Sometimes I forget how people who aren't part of my production world might perceive this funny business. This husband and wife were not actors, nor were their children, and as a result they had no idea what laid in store for them. They never thought about what's involved in this activity.

There was no need for me to worry about under-eye circles, to contour, or to minimize aging, and all that goes along with professional on-camera personas. Sitting in my chair was a farmer who was kind enough to open up his home and share his story with strangers. I just wanted him to be comfortable and to support him, and perhaps he would be able to glean some useful material about this occurrence and share some laughs with his family when they recounted that day.

Maybe the story will go something like, "Dorothy, remember when Trista put makeup on me? She said she was just getting me 'camera-ready.' Afterwards she told me it was permanent makeup. Hahahahahaha!"

We filmed Mac and his family for an educational piece the specialized doctors would be using in their practice, for patients with this debilitating disease.

When I think of Parkinson's, my mind immediately returns to Michael J. Fox and the awareness and education his face and image have brought to this disorder. The purpose of this video was to bring awareness to a treatment that's available for those afflicted with Parkinson's. It's called DBS, or direct brain stimulation. Michael J. Fox was not a candidate for this procedure and he didn't receive the DBS treatment, but Mac did.

We were with Mac and his family to portray their decisions, talk about how the disease had affected them, and also to conduct an experiment on camera. This helpful video was to explain the risky procedure that he and his family chose to undergo.

Thin wires and electrodes had been implanted into both sides of Mac's brain in the areas that control his arm and leg movements. It might be a different location for another patient, depending on the symptoms they are addressing. Mac had hair, so I couldn't see where the electrodes had been placed. These transmit electrical signals through the wires, much like a pacemaker, which stimulate a specific region of the brain and block some signals which cause some symptoms of Parkinson's.

During our interviews, I learned about the family's decision to go ahead with the procedure of DBS. They weighed the pros and cons with the timing of the disease and the doctor's recommendations before deciding to proceed.

Mac had exhibited many of the common signs of Parkinson's. He was unable to walk and had limited use of his hands. After the placement of the electrodes, his quality of life improved. He walked, fed himself, and wasn't as limited with his physical movement—to the point I really wouldn't have known he had Parkinson's when we first met Mac.

Mac's son, who helped run the ranch, was interviewed in a hay barn before we packed our gear and headed to interview the doctors who performed the original surgery. After I got the doctors ready in their office, they also had interviews on camera about this fascinating subject and then we moved on to the experiment.

Take one: Mac walked up and down the hallway with no assistance. He did have a cane, but it was only used as precaution, should he suddenly lose his balance.

Take two: the doctor turned off the DBS electrodes with a small remote. I noticed Mac's hair was out of place. Normally, I would've whisked in and fixed it, but my job had clearly changed. I was not here just to be a makeup artist, but I was also on the sidelines silently cheering to serve as a reverent witness to a life-changing breakthrough, thanks to the dedication of those medical professionals.

I put down my hairspray and held Dorothy's hand.

Take three: with the doctor and the assistant at Mac's side, and with the electrodes turned off, Mac's hands and legs began to shake uncontrollably.

The doctor and his assistant helped Mac to his feet and he attempted to walk. Without the electrodes stimulating that part of his brain, it was impossible.

Take four: they turned the electrodes back on. Mac could walk again. A miraculous event—now that's something to cheer about.

Cheerleaders usually have spectators; in my job I have a diverse audience. God bless all you people who have the desire to be an extra. The task requires you to show up and knit a blanket or twiddle your thumbs until you get summoned to the set, just to be in the background.

Taci's friend Micaela was asked to be background for a day. Her husband is a producer and suggested she make a contribution. "Should I do it?" Micaela asked.

In unison, Taci and I both yelled into the phone, "No." Time is our most precious commodity. Do you really want to spend it being ignored?

Micaela couldn't help herself. I guess the curiosity got the best of her. She was asked to be a driver and was parked out of sight until they yelled "action." Then she drove down the block, parked out of the camera frame, and repeated, for 12 hours. Needless to say, she never volunteered again.

Some first-timers fantasize about hanging out with the stars, getting into a lively conversation with a famous actor, having lunch with the crew and cast, seeing themselves on the big screen, or the elusive prize of snapping a worthy Facebook selfie. Not going to happen.

Several years ago I was working on a national commercial and I had two leads that required massive touch-ups between each take. Celebratory confetti was shot over them while they were busting out moves. Between picking out the bits of debris sticking to their sweaty skin from the dancing and re-doing their hair, I had my hands full. We were shooting this inside an office with glass walls.

In the background were a group of individuals. Some were directed to sit at their computers and pretend they were working; others were to walk down the hallway; a few milled by the water cooler whispering about last night's sitcom. If there were no extras, it wouldn't appear realistic. Background is key. Forget what I said earlier. All who are interested come and enjoy a show of unicorns jumping over rainbows.

At the top of the day, the background folks sat in my chair and, like a revolving door, I spit them out quickly after a quick assessment that indeed they looked the part of an office worker.

After our umpteenth reset inside our dance party scene, one of the female extras insisted I re-apply her lipstick. I promised I would. Why should I? I can't see her lips. I can't even see her in the monitor. Her back is to the camera when she is filing at her desk.

Another extra asked if I could powder her. Oh, you know I will, but is it necessary? She appears way, way back, so small in the frame she could be on fire and no one would notice. The list of demands continued. Every background wanted attention.

As a cheerleader I chant, "Go, team, go! You all look fantastic." I don't dare say what's really on my mind...*I can't see you!*

I have found the most challenging cheerleading happens during weddings.

My first wedding and the ceremony was starting in 30 minutes. I waited and waited—no bride.

As the wedding march began playing, the bride finally arrived.

I was applying lipstick and mascara while her father locked arms with his daughter and their procession began. If this is the drill, I decided that bridal makeup wasn't going to be my source of gratification.

My friend Cassie told me one of her clients wanted to hire me for a wedding.

"I'm booked," I said.

"You don't even know the date yet," Cassie said.

"Did she just get engaged and it's next year?" I asked.

"Yep," Cassie replied.

"I'm booked," I avowed.

"Don't worry, she isn't a bridezilla," Cassie assured me. "It will be held at a secluded romantic winery."

"I'm in."

Unlike my first wedding experience, Brenda the bride and I met a few weeks before the big day to do a trial makeup session. I try to always do this to guarantee I have interpreted her ideas correctly. I will snap a photo, jot down notes, and set her products aside. I'm ready to do some wine tasting. I mean, I'm ready for her big day.

I arrived two hours before the wedding photos were scheduled, which was plenty of time to set up, settle in, and complete Brenda's makeup.

"Trista, my mama wants her makeup done too. Is that a possibility?" asked Brenda.

"Sure. Let's do yours first," I said.

That request was a small snowball that rolled into an avalanche.

"I want to go in a different direction with my makeup than when we did it for the trial test. I want to look like Kim Kardashian."

Brenda has red hair and fair skin. How can she ever look like Kim K.? As a cheerleader, I kept smiling.

After Brenda's hair person failed to show up—and you know what an expert I am in this department—her blood sugar dropped and she needed food, but the caterers had not yet arrived; the groom cut himself while shaving and had red nick marks I needed to conceal; and the maid of honor couldn't fit into her dress.

I called my girlfriend and seamstress, Sheri, for reinforcements and asked her to bring her sewing machine to let out the zipper. "Oh, and Sheri, bring a sandwich."

After what seemed to be an eternity of wedding cheerleading, I had waited long enough for them to bring me a Cabernet. God knows I deserved it.

*What?* No wine until after dinner is served. This cheerleader was hittin' the bricks. Trista out—mic drop!

For the next wedding I foolishly committed to, I brought Amy, Meyers, Emily, and Sheri. This head cheerleader needed a squad. Even though my glam-squad doesn't wear the same uniform and lip color and sport high ponies, we definitely all share the same desire to work as a unit.

We were hired to do the entire wedding party. After four hours of our chairs being occupied and a never-ending line of waiting men in tuxes and women in gowns, we did a final tally. We had completed makeup and hair on 32 individuals and the wedding party had only 12. Well, I guess cheerleaders love big crowds.

I no longer do weddings and Trista lived happily ever after.

Sometimes when I'm cheerleading and my team is down, I stand up and cheer a little louder.

Matt Jamie is one of my favorite producer/directors because of his paramount efforts to be a team player, and as a cheerleader I'm all about teams. As I entered the production studio, he briefed me on our project and the on-camera talker.

We were filming with the regional health district for a non-smoking campaign.

Jesse was chosen to tell her story about how she kicked the habit.

"I just want to clarify, Jesse is a girl," said Matt.

Jesse exhibited very masculine qualities. She wore a man's tie and her hair was shaved on both sides. She had a stiff dose of product on the top of her hair and it flared with attitude. She had rosacea, an affliction causing the skin to exhibit redness. Most of us have a little pinkness in our skin, but Jesse's was serious. I knew it would be tricky to address.

"Have you ever had makeup done, Jesse?"

"No, never. I'm a nervous wreck. I wish I hadn't agreed to torture myself this way. I woke up with a big red pimple smack between my eyes and I wish at this very moment it were a bullet instead."

"Take a deep breath, Jesse. I'll be taking care of you today, and let's erase the word nervous and replace it with excited."

She looked at me strangely. "Aren't you just going to throw some powder on me, before I get my ass whipped in front of the camera?" Jesse asked.

"When we wrap, you'll be glad you colored outside the lines."

"Huh?"

"You know, do something outside of your comfort zone," I said.

"I've never heard anything described that way." Jesse paused.

"I got you covered, and your skin." While we talked, I applied a green primer to neutralize the redness in her skin tone. My biggest concern was her perception. Since she doesn't wear makeup, how would she ever understand the green goop I smeared on her face? My conversation was like creating a distraction while ripping off a Band-Aid. "It's gone. No one will see it now."

"Trista, what do you think of these glasses?"

A question warranting an opinion can be considered a sign of trust. "Do you need them to walk and talk?" She put them back in her pocket.

"Do you like my tie?" Jesse gave it a tug.

"It's perfect." As long as it's "straight," but that's tongue-in-cheek. I didn't want her makeup to look too girly. Nothing too bright or pink. I thought mascara might be pushing it, but I added a skosh and did the top lashes only and finished with a soft beige lip color.

"You're going to nail this, Jesse. Matt the interviewer is super cool. How many people can say they were part of a video? This will be an experience you won't forget. A good story to share later."

"I'm going to look like a total blubbering idiot." Her head tilted downwards.

"Do you have a best friend who makes you feel completely safe?"

"Emersyn. Why?"

"Follow me." I escorted Jesse into the filming studio where Matt, Tomas the cameraman, Noah the assistant, and the Regional Health District clients were waiting.

"Doesn't she look great, guys?" There was no response. I was hoping for an "ooh" or an "ahh," so that reinforced my need for louder cheerleading.

Matt was sitting next to the camera to direct Jesse with the questions.

"Just be yourself, Jesse, and pretend you are having a conversation with Emersyn. Matt and the camera are now Emersyn." I whispered to her while I got her set on her mark in front of the bright lights and camera.

"You're right. I can do this." Jesse exhaled.

I stood directly in her eye-line directly behind the camera, which normally is a big no-no. I knew at that point she was comfortable with me and she knew I had her best interests at heart. I wanted her to see a smiling, friendly face when she was telling her story.

"I started smoking when I was a teenager because my friends did it and I was mad at my mom," Jesse began. She explained the long journey she had taken, quitting over and over again. She also developed breathing difficulties. Her throat was getting dry and she started to cough.

"Take a drink of water," said the client.

"No, I don't want to mess up my lipstick." Jesse smiled.

"That's why I'm here. Give me something to fix." I touched up her lips, while she laughed. That's when I knew she liked her new look. Even though I had shown her in the mirror before we got onto the stage, I wasn't sure until that moment.

Jesse continued with her story. "I quit smoking because I hated the way I smelled. I started dating a girl who didn't like smoking, so I did it for her, but it didn't work. My advice for those of you watching is to only do it for yourself. When I learned that key piece, that's when it stuck. I was bored and needed to replace my behavior with my hands so I used a clicker pen every time I had the desire to smoke. It's been years since I smoked and I will never light up again."

After the interview, Tomas took still photos of her for the campaign and when we wrapped, the client told Jesse they would send copies of the pictures.

"Oh, good, I will frame one and give it to my mama. It will be the closest she's seen me to being a girl."

I was leaving for a hotel to work with some dignitaries flying in for a fundraiser dinner show and my phone rang. I was pressed for time but picked up the call without even giving it a second thought.

"Hello, Trista. You don't know me, but I have a special favor I need from you," the women on the other end said.

"Well, I'm not sure..." I was hesitant as my mind flashed back to Jerry/Jerianne and the transgender makeover.

"My daughter has a rare form of cancer and she only has months to live. She has one wish."

Okay, she got my attention.

"Nena wants to marry her high school sweetheart today. Can you please find it in your heart to make time for her?"

Nena and her mom arrived at the hotel suite where Amy, Meyers, and Emily were preparing the entourage of show guests.

I hugged Nena tightly as if I had known her forever. Because of the cancer treatments Nena had no hair, eyebrows, or eyelashes.

"I just want to be pretty today," Nena said sweetly.

Marcy Few, wife of Mark Few, the head coach of the Gonzaga men's basketball team, was leading the soirée and was my next scheduled client. Marcy is gorgeous, and graciously stepped aside while I attended to Nena.

I applied false lashes and colored in some brows. We airbrushed and used a soft palette of colors to help her feel like the beautiful bride she was.

The event was for Coaches versus Cancer. Nena was 17 and passed away later that year. This was not a fairytale.

Way back when, Seattle had an NBA basketball team, the Supersonics. The team was rallying the public to fund construction of a new arena in Seattle. I was part of the production crew to do a push campaign to keep the team from leaving.

They chose Lenny Wilkens to be a spokesman, a perfect man to save the team because he was a former player and coach for the Sonics. Wilkens also received a gold medal as head coach for the men's national basketball team at the Olympics. He was an NBA champion, Coach of the Year, and Hall of Fame player. He was an inaugural inductee into the college basketball Hall of Fame. He also received the highest honor with the retirement of his Sonics jersey, number 19. When I met Lenny Wilkens at a fire station to shoot his plea for mercy, I was weak in the knees and thought I was going to faint. I've met Hollywood mega icons and not been star-struck, but when it comes to sports figures: fireworks. I get tongue-tied. Yeah, right? Me, at a loss for words? It should seem natural. After all, I'm a cheerleader.

While Wilkens talked into the camera, I hung on his every word and I was sad to move on to another scene where circus performers literally were hanging.

We filmed a birthday party in a park where one of the star Sonics players crashed the festivity. It never snows in downtown Seattle. It was snowing in downtown Seattle. I went to buy hot chocolate for the unprepared team to cheer them on while we worked in freezing temperatures.

We moved our squad inside and finished the commercial with a pie-throwing contest. They gave me a ladder to apply the makeup on the seven-foot basketball players.

The campaign ultimately failed, and the Sonics were sold and became the Oklahoma Thunder. Even though Seattle was left without an NBA basketball team, we have the Seahawks to cheer on to victory.

The Seahawks needed me for a pre-game video introduction of their players. Each team member would say their name into the camera and say where they were from. I had my director's chair set up, and plenty of oil de-shine product when the first linebacker arrived. He looked at my chair and my sprawled-out kit.

"No way, man," the linebacker said.

"Hi, I'm Trista, I'm here to do your makeup."

"Get out of here." He turned and exited.

In strolled the next player.

"Hi, I'm Trista, here to do a little touch-up." Out he went.

In came the next. "Hi, I'm Trista, just a quick..."

No go.

Next...

"Hey, great game Sunday. That one-handed catch in the end zone to tie the game, wow, Steve, you rock, man."

"Oh, thanks...your name?"

"Trista. Thank you for doing this. I'm here to get you in front of the camera." I reached for an anti-shine sheet. He sat in my chair but it was snug. He was a smaller running back. I could see why those bigger 300-pounders wouldn't sit in this chair.

After I prepped Steve, I took off the back and the arms of my director's chair; still not going to work. I scrounged up an oversized love seat from the lounge area before the next player.

"Hey, hey, what do you know? Excited to pound those Bears on Sunday?" I asked.

"Oh, you know it," said the receiver.

He pulled his head away when I went in with the powder puff. "It's okay. Let me show you something." I put the mirror up. "It's only for the camera to see, it's invisible."

Next player.

"If you don't like it you can wash it off."

He looked in the mirror. "It's okay."

I got through the entire lineup only because I can speak "football."

Mark Few, the head coach of the Gonzaga men's basketball team, was to be featured in *USA Today* magazine.

"Trista, when I was a kid we didn't use sunscreen. I have a lot of sun damage," said Mark. I didn't care. I wanted him to sit in my chair forever. I will address any and all skin issues on Mark in trade for a private interview to ask him his thoughts on March Madness and the ability to make it to the Final Four. Instead, I continued on to a subject that wouldn't cause me to become overly excited and stammer.

"How are Marcy and the kids?"

Moving on, I was hired for an anti-climactic project with *Weight Watcher Magazine.* They flew in a photographer, director, costumer, and interviewer from New York. We toured the state and documented several weight-loss success stories to publish in their national magazine

We arrived at Mary's beautiful home on the west side of Washington. It was a busy household with dogs barking, kids playing, and with every knock on the door the German family became larger. Parents and friends were stopping by. The word was out. This was a big day at the Mary home. How often does it happen in your lifetime that you are asked to be in a national magazine?

Working out of a home has a few obstacles, but I much prefer this to my location last month—I had been on top of a mountain trying to apply frozen makeup during a blizzard. Yes, I prefer the comforts of home. I scored a location for my station. I wouldn't need to cart my set bag. This house was the set.

"Mary, I'm ready whenever you are," I said.

"Oh, my. I've never had a makeover done before. I'm so excited. I watch the *Today* show, where they do those makeover ambushes, with Hoda and Kathy Lee."

"Ma, Ma, come over and see what Trista is doing. Wait, Trista, let me put the dogs out...Dad, get Max. Pauly, you gotta take that noisy toy out of here. I told you once, twice." Mary rushed to her son, Pauly.

"Okay, Trista, I'm ready. Ma, Ma, let's put those veggies out for these nice people," Mary said. I heard her mother's voice from the kitchen.

"Where are they, Mary? Do you want these fruit trays out? What food do you want me to put out, Mary?

"Oh, excuse me." Mary left and headed to her mother. "Ma, just put it all out. These people have come a long way, I'm sure they are hungry."

"What about the bread I made yesterday, and the cookies, and the tortellini?" her father asked.

"Dad, hush, this is Weight Watchers," Mary scolded. "Trista, I'm coming."

"It's okay, Mary, no rush." Mary was a moving target so I went quickly to use the powder room. I discovered the grossest "toidy" untidiness. I couldn't do an about-face and exit. Someone would see me leaving and assume I was the cause. I traded my cheerleader uniform for a janitor jumpsuit. I searched for cleaning supplies under the sink and addressed the mess. Eek, note to self: inspect before entering.

Mary plopped down in the dining room chair. Her husband, Monty, yelled from upstairs. "I can't find the shirt you wanted me to wear, Mary. Mary, what do you want me to do?"

Mary and the wardrobe costumer raced up the stairs. The rest of the crew was scouting through the house, debating on locations.

Mary took a big gulp of air as she finally sat in my chair. Her brows were as thick as her accent and Mary's large pore size prevented her from being a good candidate for airbrush. But she was really looking forward to experiencing the new contraption. So I prepped her skin to shrink the pore size with a skin toner. I used what she thought was a moisturizer but really was a pigmented foundation to camouflage flaws. Then I airbrushed over the top to meet her expectations. Added some color, contour, and lips.

Mary was not a makeup wearer, so I didn't want to overwhelm her taste palette. I was going for the K.I.S.S. look: Keep. It. Super. Simple.

When I had finished I gave her my hand mirror. Would she like my enhancements? Did I give her enough cheerleading during our session to gain the confidence to wear this new look?

"Ma, Dad, Monty, come quick—I'm a new woman!"

The following Weight Watchers interview was with an introverted gal. Well, anyone besides Mary was going to be shyer. When I observed the family photos on the walls of her home, Christina had white lips in every one of them, along with practically non-existent, very white-blonde eyebrows that were going to disappear on the page of a magazine. Most non-actress women are set in their ways when it comes to makeup application. The way you're taught in high school is how you continually feel comfortable when you look at yourself in the mirror. I took that into account along with her personality. I was light-handed and soft in my color choices. When I showed her the results, though, she was disturbed. This is when my job as cheerleader really comes into play, when the director is ready for a touchdown and I'm able to rally the team. The scoreboard stays at zero. I assured her the changes were necessary for the camera and the producer supported me. The crew told her how lovely she looked, but when she got in front of the camera to tell her story, she shut down. Game over.

Christina nonchalantly smudged her lips. That gave me the cue for what I needed to do. We were granted permission to leave the set.

I replicated her habitual makeup using the family photo I saw when I first entered the house and we're back in the game.

The next day we moved locations to yet another household. Celia had a large, expressive Italian family who enjoyed cooking and entertaining with food. She had gained 100 pounds after she gave birth to her last child and she struggled and compromised, but was finally able to lose all the weight she had gained. She was camera-ready, loved my makeup, and was ready to show us how she changed her eating habits by making a healthy smoothie with her family.

"Celia, when I say action, go ahead and put some veggies in the blender," the director prompted.

Celia and her family chopped up some red peppers, carrots, kale, and added some juice.

"Cut," said the director. "Okay, now I'm going to change the camera angle, go ahead and turn on the blender." Simon says, turn on the blender. Simon didn't say, put on the lid before you turn it on.

The entire family was wearing the smoothie.

"Cut."

# Behavior Analyst

In my arena, I have a front and center seat to analyze some of the most mystifying behavior. Is it learned, environmental, or are we just plain psycho? Spend one day in a circus and you would know it's all three.

I had a request to work on a project that was a typical who-done-it and also about the value of true love. The shoot would run about a month in the back woods of Idaho, at an old house and barn and a few abandoned storefront structures. I had just finished a big movie and I was exhausted. I hated to say "no," because in this business it's feast or famine. I have learned to accept all job offers, but my need to be a domestic goddess was ringing louder than a paycheck. I just wanted to sleep in my own bed, eat cookies, and watch mindless television.

I had a brand new artist who had joined my team and she was chomping at the bit to fly solo. I decided this would be a great opportunity for her to do so. The requirements seemed to fit her wheelhouse. It was a small cast with minimal makeup needs and an occasional application of simple blood effects. She needed my help setting up and a little guidance on developing the look for the characters. Fair enough.

Hailey owned a personal camper, slightly bigger than a Volkswagen bug. She was bringing it to the location and planned on using it as the makeup trailer. Production was thrilled because filming in a deserted ranch town had unimaginable limitations. Any help to save them money was welcomed. October in Idaho with nowhere to hang out? Baby, it's cold. I was happy to hand this project to Hailey. My body surely wouldn't have thawed out until June.

The lead actress was in her early 20s. As a child actress, Katelyn had major success. She's beautiful and possessed an edgy non-conformist style I found interestingly untamed.

While I waited for my makeup artist, Hailey, to arrive, I bonded with Katelyn immediately. My first instinct was to mother her. She was kind and fun; the qualities I crave in any new child-parent relationship.

Katelyn would portray a sinister newlywed caught up in a murderous web. We started discussing her role and the makeup and hair ideas to pull it together. We applied dark colors under her eyes to bring out a moody sassiness her character would exhibit.

I had planned on Hailey being there for the introduction. It would've saved me time in explaining all that had transpired. Hailey's excuse was maneuvering her trailer. It wasn't easy hauling it through those back roads. I get it, but in the entertainment world it is a serious sin to be late for your call time. I tell my artists tardiness is unacceptable, unless you are in the hospital bleeding profusely, and I'm not proposing the universe support that notion by manifesting such an idea—God forbid. But hey, navigating a trailer in a foreign territory...completely plausible to have delays.

The first day Hailey and I established most of the actors' looks. The following shooting day we had a new actor flying in, so I planned on being available for Hailey, but after that I thought I'd be homebound. My *Will and Grace* reruns were waiting.

While I waited for Hailey in her trailer, the assistant director, Conner, popped in. "Trista, can we start makeup on the cast?"

"Definitely, let's start with Katelyn. Bring her in."

I searched for her kit that we'd created and it was nowhere to be found. Actually I couldn't find anyone's kit. We had been robbed. Wait, not only were the kits nowhere, but we were nowhere. Theft was unlikely. Where was my makeup artist, Hailey? She would surely shed some light on the crisis. Why hasn't she responded to my texts? I was losing my patience. On second thought, how can you lose something you don't possess? I have zero patience. I never fold my clean laundry; I just wrap my clothes in a ball and throw the ball in a basket. I don't even have the patience to sign my name. I scribble two characters and move on.

Finally, Hailey sent a text response. "I took the kits home with me last night, and then I forgot them. So sorry, kiss, hug, be there soon."

There was no way I could explain this to production. They would not understand. Had I really hired someone so inept?

Katelyn walked in disheveled and sleepy with her dark under-eye makeup still visible from the day before, a sliver of good news on that messy morning. She was messy. It matched the character she played. I could match, fix, clean up her face using my airbrush, and scavenge from other master makeup inventory to pull it off.

I continued to maneuver blindly through the cast lineup with none of our earlier test notes or products we arranged the day before.

After I had completed the cast makeup, Hailey arrived with the kits and I sent her to set to do last looks.

On our first break I had a heart to heart with Hailey.

"I didn't want the makeup to freeze; it seemed like the right thing to do," she explained.

That sounded logical and, really, this was an unusual setting. "But Hailey, you can't be late. Be an hour early, sit in your warm car, and catch up on Instagram."

She agreed to comply as Trevor, our handsome lead actor, walked by. "Hailey, you were lit at karaoke last night!"

"Thanks, Trev. A bunch of us are going to the Iron Horse after wrap. Are you down?" Hailey asked.

"Oh, you know it. I'm not sure about Katelyn though, she's in bad shape," Trevor said.

I've never been a party animal after 14 hours of shooting. I totally get the camaraderie of chuckling with workmates and friendly faces over the common stories of the day, especially when you are away from the comforts of home and without the support of loved ones. It can be lonely, but I never have the energy at the end of the day. Speaking of home, I'm sick.

"Okay, Hailey, have fun tonight but remember, in the morning, be early. I'm heading out."

I pondered Hailey's behavior as I wandered back to her trailer to get my car keys. Perhaps it's my own behavior I should question. Should I muster up my foreign emotion of patience? Hailey will come through. My bed pillow needed fluffing.

I caught a glimpse of our lead actress, Katelyn, smoking alongside the overlook to the river below. She was lying down on the dirt and her makeup appeared rougher than planned.

I rushed over to the A.D., Conner, and told him we were going to need extra time before she was in front of the camera. No sense attempting to put her together until they were ready for her.

I returned to set to give Hailey the heads-up about Katelyn and I couldn't find her. I heard the announcement for last looks and

Hailey didn't respond. That show only had the money for one artist and I had invested two days for free as a courtesy, for the love...

"Everyone settle in. Roll sound."

"Speed."

"Action."

I looked in the monitor and it was a close-up on Trevor. He had a dark smudge on his cheek camera right. Geez, had he just smoked with Katelyn? No, he's not a smoker, but this wasn't a Western film where I welcomed dusty help. I ran to find extra makeup supplies inside Hailey's trailer and grabbed a sponge, a tissue, a brush, and some powder.

As I returned I heard the director say, "Cut," I dashed in and fixed Trevor without an invite.

I saw Hailey in another room and she was laughing with some of the cast off camera. I gave her the "what's up" shrug and she turned away.

"Trista, Katelyn is on camera soon, I will send her your way," said Conner. Why didn't he summon Hailey?

Katelyn entered the trailer in worse shape than earlier. From what I concluded, her hangover hadn't diminished.

"What color combination should we go with?" Katelyn dug through her purse.

"We need to keep the continuity, so no change on colors."

"See all these choices?" She displayed her pillbox for me.

Oh, she wasn't referring to lipstick and eye shadow...dear lord.

"I definitely need an Adderall for focus." She picked out a sorted array of colors with different shapes and sizes. She snapped them in her mouth and with one quick tilt of her head they disappeared. Oh, no, this wasn't happening.

That wasn't my first experience with substances and actors. On one of my first films I saw white particles around the nostrils of my actor while he sat in my makeup chair. I reasoned it must be from a powdered donut he just munched on. The next morning I saw the same residue. I made a mental note that he was a scrappy eater and to be on the lookout. I'm on this. Where were those tasty pastry morsels anyway? I didn't see them on the craft service table. Is he hiding them with his personal stash? Why is it by his nose and not his mouth? I was so naive.

I remembered another film when my lead actor, John, was on a call with his attorney while I was doing his makeup for the first time. He had just arrived into town and we were doing a camera test.

"What do you mean you can't take care of this?" John asked. "I understand there is a warrant, but I'm shooting for a few months." He ended the call and then hit the speaker button and reached his wife's voicemail. She too was in the entertainment business. Pamela was more successful than her husband, and was the winner of an Academy Award. He exploded. "She never takes my calls!" I thought his behavior might be the result of stress, but I learned otherwise.

Days into our schedule we were shooting a late night scene where John's car crashed through a store window. A stunt driver performed that. After each take, John needed to start at his "mark," the first spot where the camera rolled. His first "mark" was at the car door.

When the director yelled "action," that was his cue to open the door and get in the car.

Simple, except John could not physically do it.

At first you could hear small giggles from the crew, then it became more serious. It's part of the scene, so it's not like someone can run in and open the door for him. After we ran behind shooting schedule, we wrapped without finishing the scene. We were notified of a three-day unscheduled vacation.

The actor had to sober up so we could continue filming. The insurance bond paid for the budget overages.

When John returned, I presumed he had dried up. When he entered, he threw his phone onto my workspace and my powders spewed everywhere. "Do ya know what I had for breakfast Trista? *Iriiiish coooffeeeee.*"

He argued with me belligerently, slurring that the scars I was applying were on the wrong side, even after I showed him pictures of the placement.

I had other artists hold his drunken ass still so I could do his makeup to meet my shooting deadlines. He disputed and quarreled about everything. John and alcohol caused me serious angst.

Back to Katelyn. I watched her ingest her kaleidoscope of pills, and afterwards she passed out lying on top of a picnic table. I saw her long blond hair peeking out from under a tarp she used as a blanket.

Conner called her name to report to set.

If I had to wager, I would've bet against her.

Without hesitation, Katelyn got in front of the camera and delivered a flawless performance. It was a good thing we weren't in Vegas.

That was a suitable time for my exit.

The producer, Jim, stopped me seconds before my getaway. Was it Groundhog Day? "The actors don't feel comfortable having Hailey do their makeup. What will it take for you to stay on this show?"

We negotiated a contract and I asked we keep Hailey as an unpaid intern. In other words, she could party on, with no responsibilities, but more importantly I didn't want to embarrass her. We wouldn't have to change her title. She could save face. Oh, and can I put in an addendum to request my bed and bonbons?

I scouted for Hailey to inform her of the change. It didn't go well. Hailey cried hysterically as she handed out her cell number to all the actors. The show shut down during her dramatic exit. I was confused about my artist's intentions. Observing her behavior, I surmised it wasn't the partying that caused this road to be bumpy. She used to be an actress and that was a bigger motivation than pursuing makeup. The main importance for Hailey was to connect with the actors and their agents. After she was assured the actors would help her with new job leads, she hitched up her trailer bug and exited in a plume of dust, faster than the Roadrunner in the cartoon.

I wanted to renegotiate my negotiated contract with a provision for an electric blanket and a fireplace. My new makeup studio was now a barn.

Several days passed, and Katelyn shared her personal story.

Her mother had taken her money from her childhood movie successes and bought herself a house. While Katelyn struggled financially, it appeared her family was taking advantage of her. To numb her pain, she took pills.

One early morning, Katelyn cried. "I quit. I hate this movie." Her black makeup streamed down her cheeks and she wrestled through her purse.

"I'm right there with you, sweetie," I said while comforting her. "I quit, too. Drinking water, that is. There is no running water and I refuse to use the outhouse."

I was the only one laughing while she searched for her water bottle to wash down her multi-colored pills. She then left to seek out her tarp.

Jim the producer rushed toward me. "Katelyn is out of control. I just got word she wants to fly home."

As a behavior analyst veteran, I had studied Katelyn's patterns. "Jim, just wait 20 minutes. Her rainbow will kick in."

When I witness an actor struggling with substances, I feel a case of exhaustion coming on, except that wasn't the situation when I worked with Calvin Cordozar Broadus Jr., a.k.a. "Snoop Dogg" and his very large entourage.

His sister was his hairdresser (even though he had cornrows that never changed), his uncle was his chef, and then I'm not sure of the relationship with "Bishop." He walked around with a very large caldron of special X-rated brew.

Also included in the posse was Snoop's dog pound of bodyguards who were worth lots if they were paid by the pound. Every night the posse would descend upon the streets of the city to find large-breasted women who would hang out in Snoop's smoke-filled trailer.

"Do you know what today is, Trista?" Snoop was texting on his phone as I was finishing his makeup.

"No, I sure don't."

"Today is my birthday."

"Oh my gosh, Snoop, happy birthday!"

The next morning Snoop settled into the makeup chair and asked, "Trista, do you know what today is?"

"No, please tell me."

"It's my birthday."

"Snoop, I thought yesterday was your birthday?"

"Every day is my birthday, Trista, every day." Snoop smiled.

I guess those women were his presents. My biggest birthday present would've been the knowledge I was switched at birth.

Even though he smoked pot, Snoop was professional and chill. True dat.

There was this unforgettable movie I shot with Taci in the early summer of 2009, with kind, talented Brittany Murphy. She brought her husband Simon, her mama Sharon, and her adorable dog. Our base was in Eugene, Oregon, and one of our filming locations was along the gorgeous McKenzie River. For added kicks, Taci and I created our own entertainment. We initiated a game of incognito: who will ultimately identify us as a mother-daughter duo? Taci was careful to substitute "Trista" for "Ma," which was entertaining in itself.

When I learned Brittany's husband Simon was going to be the makeup artist for Brittany on that project, I was astonished. No one was aware Simon was an artist. He had no prior experience. Is he a natural? Perhaps he had been doing his wife's hair and makeup personally and wanted to start building a résumé. After

I set Simon up with some basic tools, like a hairbrush, he was appointed a makeup/hairstylist.

On set, Simon stared straight ahead at all times, as if everyone was invisible. He never watched the monitor or engaged in conversation. Was he nervous? Shy? He was a foggy noggin.

A couple days into our schedule, while I was in my makeup trailer getting my co-lead actors ready, the director, Darin, summoned me to set.

I was led to the monitor while Brittany rehearsed.

"Fix Brittany's lips," said Darin.

They couldn't get Simon to understand the problem. It was like production was talking a language he couldn't possibly comprehend. Simon had taken a tube of lipstick and drawn heavy comedic clown-type red around her entire lip area. Simon definitely took a wrong turn, but I wanted to stay in my own lane.

Not only was Simon in bad shape, but Brittany, too, had some issues. She was super thin. I've never seen elbows that tiny.

The art director had to find smaller chairs for her to sit in and cups to drink from, to hide her size. She also had problems getting out of a chair. She appeared like a newborn doe whose legs were not developed and ready to stand quite yet.

There was a scene where she was to carry her "child" across a street. She physically couldn't do it. There is so much emphasis on thinness in Hollywood, and the media pounces on unflattering pictures to plaster on magazine covers. As an actress there is a lot of pressure on your appearance, and I'm sure it causes insecurities.

I don't know the reasons why Brittany was so thin, but she had her mama, Sharon, with her. Doesn't that equate to warm chocolate cookies and milk?

On the day we wrapped with Brittany, she held up her little doggie as she waved, giggled, and gave accolades to cast and crew. She really was a sweetheart.

At the same time, Taci and I wrapped up our own little masquerade game and crowned ourselves victorious.

In December, a few months after we finished, Brittany passed.

*Something Wicked* was the last movie Brittany shot. I always wondered while we filmed if she was healthy.

Five months after Brittany died, her husband Simon passed also. It was so overwhelmingly tragic and I found it to be very mysterious.

Returning to Katelyn, I was worried based on my past experiences with actors and their abuses. I wanted to bake her motherly chocolate chip cookies, hire a therapist, and make all her past problems go away. She deserved it, but as a behavior analyst I have my limitations.

After Katelyn's threats to abandon ship, production gave us a trailer, a brand new one with a small bedroom. We were instructed not to use the bathroom because the trailer was just a loaner and had to be returned to the dealership. To hell with that request. Hook us up. I'm dehydrated.

I had finished the morning makeup and was headed to set when Jim popped in. Oh no. Is he going to lock the bathroom door and throw away the key?

"The art department just informed me it's your job to create the big diorama scene tomorrow after Harry and Shelly are killed and they become dead body art pieces."

"To apply the blood?" I furrowed my brow. When I read the script I asked about the diorama. Usually anything applied to skin is makeup. I was assured my job consisted of pouring gallons of blood on the actors immediately before they announce "action" and that's it.

"No, you will create the missing eyes on 'Harry' and the cut-out stomach on 'Shelly.'"

"I need to hire more help, Jim." I've done mangled bodies, executions, and slit throats. I could figure this out with time and practice, but I'd been given neither. New quid pro quo: please throw in shots of tequila to my contract.

I went to check on my actors and then headed to the shack where the art department was holed up. On the door was a handwritten sign. "Stay the fuck out. Unless you're Trista." I wasn't sure how to process that. They're an unapproachable group, but I would've busted the door down without permission rating my fury. They obviously knew I was coming.

"Sorry, this movie is quite the undertaking," the art director stated.

"Tell me about it. I'm changing my job title to undertaker, caretaker, or just taker me away, like the Calgon commercial."

After discussing the direction on the dead people art diorama, I sent out a 9-1-1 distress call to my sisteress, Amy, and another artist, Kara, who did theater special effects.

My dotkin was no longer on my speed dial. Taci had graduated with a master's degree in occupational therapy and was in high demand healing patients, instead of healing the deranged world of entertainment.

We pulled it off. We airbrushed their exposed skin a bluish, grayish, death-white. We used mortician's wax and carved out absent eyes, and bought butchered raw meats to use as guts.

Our actors appeared gruesome with missing body parts.

Amy and Kara owned it. Katelyn followed. Every take, every scene, she knew her lines and delivered.

Several years after that show, I redirected my thoughts to Katelyn as I finally curled up in my comfy bed next to my fireplace sipping a hot toddy. She hasn't completed any other movies. Katelyn was such a gifted actress. What is stopping her? Is she an example of how childhood stardom can mess you up, or can she not get over her rainbow?

There are circumstances where I'm hired to be nothing other than support staff, a makeup assistant. This was the case for a television show that had been running for several seasons when I was asked by the union to fill in for a few weeks.

I traveled an entire day, parked my car at the designated parking area, and was shuttled to the makeup trailer on the busy movie lot. I had not met anyone, and I'd only had a brief phone call and a text message. It was raining. I knocked on the door.

The head of the makeup department was sitting and used her foot to open the door. I wasn't asked to come in. No greetings or introductions; I was just tossed a kit and told to go to stage three, and she pointed out the direction while the door shut.

One of the leads came over and instructed me on my last looks duties. She sized me up with a look of discernment. I actually thought I saw her nose turn upward as she was thinking, *Do you sell makeup at Rite Aid and now you think you are a movie makeup artist?*

On the set I ran into a long-time friend who worked as the prop master. He filled me in.

The original head of the makeup department was on maternity leave, so they'd brought in a substitute. Then they'd had a revolving door of artists come and go. Everyone within the department was struggling to keep their positions and were busy watching their backs. He advised me to toughen my skin and keep my nose to the grindstone. "Gotcha." I had all the answers I needed to survive.

I worked three episodes with the unhappy department. I was offered a different gig two states away and I was ecstatic to leave. As a behavior analyst, I know when to run.

Another time, I was hired for a film with Irene, a department head who came along to all the projects that Ronald, the director, worked. Irene was a woman who never delegated. That project had several makeup effects and she didn't want to share kudos.

One morning they scheduled a blood gag using a sucking device from a supply of blood at the end of tubing. The clear tube was placed through the stunt man's hair and when "action" was called, the blood would squirt profusely from his head, creating the effect of a shocking horrific wound from a gunshot.

This wasn't scripted; it was a last-minute request from the director, so there had been no rehearsals.

"Can I help you, Irene?"

"No," Irene said.

"Want to borrow my coat?" Irene was wearing a beautiful white down coat. I always wear black. You know what can happen if you wear white, especially if you are flying and in her case, solo.

"Action," said the A.D.

I watched from behind the monitor waiting for the flashing stream of burgundy red horror. Nothing.

"Cut."

"Let's go again. Quiet, everyone. Settle in, and action."

Take two, cut, and still nada.

"Makeup, makeup, what's going on?"

Out comes Irene from her crouched, hidden position, holding her tubing, looking like the last scene from the movie *Carrie*.

As a behavior analyst I say it was predictable. Preventable. For the duration of the show she wore faded scarlet bloodstains.

On my next job I analyzed sexual behavior and wondered if movie sets come with a different set of rules.

"Trista, I can't work today. You put makeup on me and I will cry rivers." Fransesca, my Italian actress, was dabbing her nose.

"Why, Fransesca?" My thoughts instantly go to arranging ice packs for swollen eyes. Ryan, my lead actor, walked into the trailer, and Fransesca fell apart and ran out.

"Do you know what's going on with Fransesca?" I asked Ryan.

"She got upset when I told her I'm not leaving my girlfriend for her."

"What? Back up." I knew Ryan was in a committed relationship and it wasn't with Fransesca.

"When we arrived a few days before filming, we got together to talk about our husband and wife characters," Ryan said.

"Yeah...and?"

"Well, we had drinks. One thing led to another and we practiced the bedroom scene in my hotel room."

"Uh-oh. You slept with her? Once?" I asked, already knowing the answer.

"Damn it, Trista, I've been sleeping with her for weeks, okay? I thought she understood. It's just sex."

I dickered with production to schedule their makeup sessions at separate times. In a short time she had fallen deeply in love with Ryan. Francesca thought sex meant relationship and she was hurt. Ryan didn't understand the emotional distress from Francesca, and thought sex was a noncommittal sport. As in any sport, there is one winner and a clear loser.

During the show I had endless situations fixing messy eye makeup from unscripted crying and heart-to-heart conversations to get her through the game.

During movie making, it's like living together and becoming an instant family. Ryan's boundaries got blurred, and Francesca got blindsided, but we managed to get through it like any dysfunctional family.

I wrapped with Ryan and Francesca and headed to the opulent Peninsula in Santa Monica.

I met with Robert Heiman, the founder of Epicuren Discovery, a skincare brand repeatedly requested by my celebrities, but I had been unable to purchase Epicuren because of its exclusivity. What, me deprived of lotions and potions? This elusive product was available to trained distributors only, and my curiosity was piqued.

After my initial introduction to Robert, he agreed to meet again in Laguna Beach, next to his headquarters. Did this mean I would be granted access to his secret products? I also was bewildered as to why Robert, an engineer, chose skincare to be his life quest. I'd always analyzed the behavior of my actors and now I was about to do the same with Robert.

My daughter Lindsey joined me, upon my insistence. "It is rare in our lifetimes to witness pure genius-ness," I said to my dotkin.

We went to The Sands, and sat next to an open window at the bar. We were so close to the ocean during high tide the waves actually splashed onto our table. Robert shared his story with Lindsey and me. He surrounded himself with a Nobel winning conglomerated team of world-renowned gurus. They conducted skin studies at the Houston burn center and discovered an enzyme found inside the cheek lining. Holy Moses, who thinks about mouth enzymes?

"Throughout our lives, the inside of our mouths never show signs of aging. So this enzyme is the heart of the Epicuren skincare," Robert explained. We were soaking up his knowledge like the waves were soaking our table linens.

"No wonder my stars request your products."

Robert also revealed he had Vitiligo, a disease affecting many parts of his body. Oh snap! My job as Robert's behavior analyst was now complete. His mission in life was to find a cure for Vitiligo, which occurs when the cells that produce melanin die or stop functioning and you lose pigmentation. "Vitiligo causes me stress and makes me self-conscious, even though it's not life-threatening or contagious," Robert said. "Michael Jackson also suffered from this exact same ailment."

"I thought Jackson lost pigmentation because he bleached his skin?"

"No, no, that's not true. MJ's dark skin turned blotchy and white. He then used makeup to even it out."

Robert knew my connections with big league actors and offered me a certification class to use the special enzymes. He was also developing an airbrush makeup line and wanted my input. I was honored and felt privileged. Well, mainly I was just glad my deprivation was over.

After my training, I added Epicuren to my repertoire of choices in the makeup trailer. Yippee Skippy. Filming with high-definition cameras. Hello, you need to address the skin.

A year after my introduction to Robert Heiman and Epicuren, I couldn't tell you what city I was in or what project I was on. My sail was at half-mast. I had finished my umpteenth person without a break and I robotically applied "Izzy" pink lip color to everyone. Was living in the fast lane taking its toll? Had I lost my mojo? The highlight of my day was not illuminating a cheekbone, but it was climbing into my bed every night. Even my actor's questions seemed identical, along with my canned answers. It was just a different face asking.

"Oh, what a fun job you have. How did you get started?" the perky actress asked.

"I woke up one day with a powder brush in my hand."

"Ooh, I bet you travel to some awesome places. What was your favorite?" said the last 444 actors.

"My backyard, because I didn't get lost going home," I said.

"How long have you been doing this?"

"Today is my first." The look on their faces was priceless.

"Who is the most famous person you have done makeup on?"

"You, of course," I say without hesitation.

"Can you come to my house every morning?"

"Definitely, it would be my pleasure." Not.

Help me...the entertainment business was extracting the living life out of me. I was fake loving everyone, not just Taci's dogs.

I don't believe in coincidences and coincidentally I received a special invitation: a retreat at Two Bunch Palms Resort in Desert Hot Springs hosted by Robert Heiman. It was Robert's turn to analyze my behavior.

Robert invited a dozen guests from all walks of life and fascinating careers. He was conducting research for a book on reshaping our approach to thought processes. Sharing in the workshop experiment was Greg Mooers, a monk who spent 15,000 hours within eight years meditating; Leslie Sloane, an alchemist, master healer, and internationally recognized author on color therapies; Ellen Shaw, Robert's sister, who wrote a book about this workshop; Elizabeth, a TV personality; Renee, a psychotherapist; Laz, a corporate lawyer, along with several others.

Robert created a labyrinth along the water's edge with lit candles and numerous bottles of all colors, shapes, and sizes. Inside, each bottle had its own unique word. We were anointed with a holy ash Leslie had brought back from her recent visit to Egypt. We were instructed to walk in our bare feet in silence down the maze path and when a bottle chose you, the first one emitting a connective energy, you were to take that bottle back to your room.

The silence continued through the evening with no music, television, social media, or phones. That by itself was an exercise.

There I was, alone with my bottle and my word, left to sit and contemplate the word "flower."

After my mind wondered aimlessly about thoughts that had nothing to do with flowers, I endeavored to make my maiden voyage of meditation. There was a flower pattern on my favorite jacket. Oh, which reminded me, it had a wine stain that needed to be removed. Flower, hmm, bees, bee stings, honey. *Focus,* I reminded myself. Flower, what is my favorite one? Well, tulips, but they don't last long. I struggled. In addition to the obviousness of the uniqueness and beauty of each, what is so special about a damn flower? Needless to say, I got off track easily, not with the normal commotions of life, but distractions from my own mind. I grabbed my sweater and pretended it was a flower. Okay, too far of a stretch. I went outside and picked a bright yellow flower from the manicured landscape. I'm sure I did something illegal. Hopefully the lawyer wasn't watching me. Meh, it's probably a weed.

I tortured myself with thoughts of that same lawyer, along with the monk, writer, healer, and others who would have profound meanings about their words and when it was my turn to discuss my flower, I would be talking about my wine-stained dry cleaning, dead tulips, and a yellow weed. I shook my head and tried easing my fears. How hard can it be truly to immerse with this flower and how does this stupid exercise free me from filing for emotional bankruptcy?

I started to quiet my thoughts by taking deep, slow, rhythmic breaths. Four deep inhales through the nose and the same number of exhales out the mouth. I think I saw something on the internet about that, or maybe it was from my doctor. No, who needs a doctor when you have Google? But I can't check right now, that would be cheating.

What did I know about breath? Well, I hold mine most of the time waiting for the next emergency while I allow everything and everyone to dictate my inner universe. I had faked a snore breath when I was saving my life lying with the lion. I used breath techniques when I was giving Michael's eulogy. I take deep breaths before I cope with my actors' appearance anxieties. I lost my breath after I was drugged in a casino. After I started the slow breathing, I followed with not allowing anyone, or any thoughts, to enter my space. I fell into a deep state of calm, and when my thoughts centered on only the flower and my breathing, I knew at that moment what I needed to learn and why I was there.

The next morning, we all gathered and when it was my turn I said, "Getting a sense of things is all about breath. I can't be anywhere except in the present moment when I'm in breath. If I'm breathing the fragrance of a flower and my focus is precisely on that, it allows me to get the sense of the moment."

"Trista, being aware of the power of now maintains your balance. Bad stress creates energy that has nowhere to go. You can change anything by redirecting your energy." As Robert spoke, he somehow seemed taller to me.

I learned my *one* life was being sliced into smithereens and sucking me dry. Only I can control how I spend my precious dynamism. I felt a renewed sense of self, health, and was glad I had made it out of my spin cycle.

After my unusual and refreshing encounter with Robert, I was hired to do a photo shoot. Our setup would be demonstrating yoga poses with the model Tiffany, along the banks of the picturesque Snoqualmie River in a national park outside of Seattle. Unbeknownst to the crew, a very prominent Chinese dignitary, along with the secret service, had tied up the traffic in Seattle. Another obstacle we faced was the inability to plug in a specific address into our GPS maps. How do you type in "Take me to the middle of nowhere?" When I arrived, some of the crew were driving in loops, lost inside the park. I was one of the first to reach our destination which, given my driving record, I would say was miraculous. I hiked onto some large boulders next to the shore and eventually meandered onto a rock in the middle of the river, where I sat and listened to the waterfall.

As I sat amid Mother Nature's finest, holding my last looks bag for Tiffany, I reflected on my outlandish life I have fought for and how much I have changed.

My zany existence has been unconventional. I've been knocked down unthinkable times and questioned my professional calling. I contemplated quitting, but I repeatedly got back up and placed one baby step in front of the next. Sometimes I'd make no steps at all but at least I was standing and seeking to find the funny lining. I've had stifling fears of how I will be treated by my next actor, producer, or director and if I'd be hired again, but here I am, an honorary circus survivor of all things chaotic.

If I had the ability to hit the rewind button of my life and was given a "take two," I wouldn't modify or reprogram anything, including my arduous childhood and #MeToo madness. It's all part of me wrapped up into who I am now.

The best is yet to come for my career, where I will continue to serve others. Is it enough? Am I enough? Yes, we all are.

The cultural landscape within the film industry is evolving, albeit a trickling progress. My biggest hope for our future is for all daughters to never fall prey to lions under any circumstances and if we encounter toothy situations, we press the pause button and simply breathe while we cling onto the courage to speak freely, with no fear of any negative consequences. We can't amend the past but with continuous dialogue, together we can shine a spotlight of awareness to eliminate inappropriate behavior and harassment.

I was completely immersed with the rock on the river tucked inside a backdrop of breathlessness in an inimitable moment of gratitude for my proudest accomplishments: my daughters. The light was vanishing, and with stillness I watched the most serene of all sunsets. My wild life of artistry completes me.

# Magician

*Here are a few things in my bag of tricks:*

### #1 Lip Service

Never mind the incredible screenplay, flashy lights, and beautiful wardrobe. Those lips—they need to be perfect. Here's my scrub to achieve perfection: teaspoon of brown sugar, a drop of honey (to seal in moisture), a splash of pure coconut oil, a sprinkle of cinnamon, and a skosh of almond oil. Use a toothbrush or fingertip and let the mixture sit as a mask or scrub. I purposefully color outside the lines so I won't deprive any skin of this goodness. You're welcome.

### #2 Do My Lashes Make Me Look Fat?

For an easy-to-master glamor lash trick, add strip false lashes under your lashes, not on top. Measure the strip length and cut excess from the outside. Add a thin line of glue on the topside of false lash strip. Steady your elbow on counter for balance and place the glued strip under your natural lashes. Align strip so there are no gaps. Tweeze false lashes together with your natural lashes and finish by adding gel liner to waterline.

### #3 Beauty Mark

A stand-alone pimple or scab becomes a star attraction when I turn it into a chocolate chip. I apply a small round circle over the top with a chocolate brown eye pencil.

### #4 Proof is in the Propolis Pudding

Emmy winning, quirky James Spader insisted on knowing the detail of every ingredient in every product I put on his skin, or within touching and smelling distance. I was cautious about everything I introduced to James and made sure I knew the facts and history. During a long, rainy, cold night in a scene with James facedown on the wet pavement, he felt achy with a scratchy throat. I treated James to a propolis tea. Propolis is an ancient healer tracing back to 350 B.C. Rich in bioflavonoids, propolis is suggested to have antibacterial, antiviral, anti-fungal, and anti-inflammatory properties. I have used it to fight infections, boost the immune system, and heal the skin.

Bees tend to be very fragile beings and when one bee gets sick they all get infected and die, so Mother Nature supports the bee community with propolis from tree buds. The resin the bees produce brushes on them as they enter the hive. The hive is as sterile as a hospital surgery unit. After several propolis teas, Spader didn't get sick.

### #5 Primp and Plump

Do you want plump, full lips without costly lip injections? Apply a small droplet of pure cinnamon oil onto the lips with cotton swabs—*only the lips*. It will sting for a few moments. No pain, no gain. Inside my makeup kit, I have lip glosses with added cinnamon oil for a quicker application. I mark a "C" with nail polish on the lid to indicate it contains cinnamon.

### #6 The Eyes Have It

Are you frustrated with lashes that clump together after applying your mascara? Before applying, comb lashes with a dry disposable mascara wand (a spoolie). This helps remove any foreign particles or dry skin. Mascara is prone to bacteria so throw it out if in doubt after a few months. Use a metal lash comb while mascara is still wet to smooth, separate, and create long perfect lashes. Do one eye at a time so mascara doesn't dry before combing lashes. Repeat mascara application with 30 quick brisk strokes to each eye.

### #7 "I'm Ready for My Close-up, Mr. De Mille."

A dermaroller or microneedle creates microscopic punctures in the skin and will boost collagen production. The results are immediate with plump, pink superficial swelling for a more youthful appearance.

### #8 Roots Be Gone

Sometimes my actors arrive with an unflattering hair problem, and I'm not talking about their tabloid photos. For a quick fix in between hair color appointments, choose a complimentary color to the brows and apply a matte eye shadow with a small, stiff makeup brush to cover the gray/roots, or do my trick: wear a hat.

### #9 Blending is my Cardio

Accentuate your beautiful features with a blended no-makeup makeup look. For liquid or cream foundation, use a damp sponge and blend below the jaw line. Blend in your blush using circular motions while smiling. Blend in your lip balm above the cheekbone as a highlighter. After your eye shadow application, use a Q-tip to smudge and create a smoky eye. Finish with a concealer (only where needed) and blend with a tinted moisturizer, eye cream, or a damp makeup sponge.

### #10 Pinch an Inch

In a pinch, use your mascara with a thin tip brush as an eyeliner. Be sure to use a waterproof mascara if your eyelids are oily, and add saline solution if your lids tend to be a little dry.

### #11 Wing It

For perfect winged eyeliner, use scotch tape to guide you. Just place the tape on both sides of the outer eye and draw perfectly straight lines.

### #12 Tear Up the Town

Desperate to eliminate your glaring shine and have no powder? Use a paper toilet seat cover. Yep, rip a piece the size of your hand and pat it on the areas needing to be rid of shine. It will not lift makeup. Repeat until you are matte.

### #13 Not a Stain on Me

I recently had an actress with a stain on her front tooth. I placed a dollop of ground turmeric with a Q-tip on the stain, waited a few minutes, rinsed, and brushed. She was ready for her close-up.

### #14 Stunt Man Relief

To ease sore muscles, take an Epsom salt bath and follow with arnica lotion.

### #15 Tone it Down

If you have a red undertone to your face, sometimes caused by the disorder rosacea, use a green primer before applying foundation to neutralize and cancel the redness. Color correcting with the appropriate shade Mac Studio Fix Powder conceals redness also.

### #16 Puppet Mouth

For women who want to minimize the lines that travel north and south of your mouth, use a lighter creamy concealer to diffuse the lines. If you look closely, the fine line is really a small darker crevice and bringing in light helps to soften it.

### #17 Nose Blind

To make a wide nose look narrower, use a darker cream foundation along the outer sides. Blend. Dark makes things look smaller. Use a highlight color down the center. Blend.

### #18 Feathery Arches

Let's get real. Brow perfection can be as individualized as the 87,000 variations at Starbucks. Perhaps my next book will be titled *Brows are Sisters Not Twins, and Sometimes a Distant Cousin.* Straight, feathered, tamed, dramatic, full, thin, microbladed, tattooed, "volumized," and au naturel are just a few choices, but if you're sitting in my makeup chair and I'm preparing you to go on camera, here are a few basic steps before I create a brow statement.

1. Brush up and down with a spoolie to remove dry skin.
2. Push up brows with wax and tweeze strays that you'll never miss.

3. Trim any wild hairs (pun intended).
4. Use Vaseline or Aquaphor to create fullness.
5. Choose a matching color to complement your brow in pencil, gel, liquid, fibers, or powder, and the correct product to achieve the look.
6. Finish with clear gel or hairspray; dry and brush again with a spoolie.

### #19 Eye-Opening

Use a straight thin-edge angled brush and a gel eyeliner to create eyes that pop. A gel dries quickly and will not smudge. Apply a very thin line from the outside to inside edge above the lashes on the lash line while delicately stretching the skin (raising your eyebrows) so there are no color gaps. Nestling the liner between the roots to create a tight line (invisible) is the key to making the eye bigger. Then do the same under the top lashes. Yes, you read that correctly. Get as close as you can under the lashes.

### #20 Hair-larious

To add hair instantly to thinning areas, use Toppik in a shade to complement your current hair color. Blow in the hair-building fibers with an atomizer to have immediately fuller hair.

### #21 Dumbo

Pin back your ears without surgery using toupeé tape.

### #22 Study Me Close

For all my makeup artist friends, take a picture of your actor with a clean face before you treat or apply any makeup. If they have acne, troubled brows, or an uneven skin tone, this is a good proof of damages. Take a second snapshot after you have perfected the look. You can zoom and get a close-up, sometimes finding mistakes before the camera test. Make changes, correct any flaw, and then take a final picture. It's also great to show the final picture as a last look to your actor for their approval.

### #23 Pucker Up

Lainie Kazan of *My Big Fat Greek Wedding* taught me this trick, and I have repeated it with all my celebrity divas.

After chugging water, the color on the lips tends to migrate north and south outside the lip line. Have a pre-wrapped straw on hand to save freshly applied lipstick. Insert bottom half of unwrapped straw into water bottle, keeping it wrapped on the tiptop, because that's classy. Attach a bobby pin sideways near the top of the wrapped straw. The bobby pin acts as a suspension to stop the straw from falling and disappearing into the bottle.

### #24 Wardrobe Malfunction No More

During the infamous wardrobe faux pas at the Super Bowl halftime show with Janet Jackson and Justin Timberlake, all that was missing was a tiny touch of medical glue to keep her undergarments from slipping. Use a little dab on the skin and press the wardrobe into place. Be sure to purchase an adhesive remover unless you plan on wearing your garb forever. Use toupee tape as a wardrobe staple. Use on a belt to keep it from slipping. Secure a man's tie onto the shirt to keep it in place. Apply on misbehaving collars and place on skin to prevent anything from moving.

### #25 Silver Screen Villains

Deep wrinkles camping out on your face? Wrinkle erasers like Retin-A, glycolics, and hyaluronic acid are products I suggest for my actors.

### #26 Poof the Puff

My actors will sleep face-up with two pillows to eliminate eye puffiness, and I use a jade eye roller with a caffeine eye cream before makeup application. The coolness of the jade and the massage helps with stagnation.

### #27 9-1-1 Shots Fired

For movies with gunfire, I keep earplugs in my arsenal. Match the actor's foundation and apply on the outside of the plug so it can't be detected. During a scene with "fire in the hole," I keep them on standby in the actor's makeup kit.

### #28 Scene Stealer

Not hitting your mark because you're anxious or ailing? That describes most of my movie stars.

Aromatherapy is one of my secret weapons. The essence of aromatherapy oil travels straight to the central nervous system, which means it works in a New York minute. If my performer is not feeling like a boss, I slay a customized therapeutic treatment to soothe their symptoms faster than Dr. Google.

There are seven ways I apply aromatherapy oils: a steam diffuser, a spray-misting bottle, topically, inhaled, infused into a facial towel, skincare products, and ingested with water or veggie capsules.

My must-have essential oil is lavender. I can feel your eyes rolling because it's overly preached, but seriously it's so intoxicating. Lavender is a sedative, anti-inflammatory, immune boosting, anti-viral, anti-anxiety skin-calming powerhouse. For a quick and easy skin application, I keep Epicuren Skin Rejuvenating Therapy in my makeup kit. It's a rich emulsion enhanced with the finest quality lavender essential oil. I dab it right under the nose or the entire face. Why be deprived?

Black pepper is another oil I keep on standby. You might think it's only used for cooking but it's a mega treatment for congestion, warming the skin, anxiety, and motivation. I had a celebrity who was trying to quit smoking and he was suffering from withdrawal. A whiff of black pepper oil from a tissue instantly suppressed his urge. He hopped to the set like an energizer bunny.

Josh Harnett wanted better mental focus and concentration. Topically applied peppermint oil was the answer. Always dilute essential oils with carrier oil before directly applying onto the skin, like coconut oil. The carrier oil will protect the skin from irritations or side effects. Hartnett rubbed his prepped peppermint wrists and deeply inhaled while he was memorizing his lines and before the director announced "action."

While filming with Peter Dinklage, I diffused a blend of peppermint and lemongrass as a bug repellent. Other ways I use peppermint is for a midday pick me up, indigestion, kissing scenes, lip plumper, and as an analgesic.

At call time I mist my makeup station and makeup brushes with sunshine and cheeriness. My spray bottle of diluted grapefruit and wild orange oils is great for uplifting moods.

Tea tree oil is by far my most popular aromatherapy because of its phenomenal healing power. It boasts of anti-cancer, anti-viral, and anti-inflammatory benefits. Mixed with benzoyl peroxide, it treats acne and because of its anti-viral qualities, it soothes cold sores. You'll find Epicuren's Anti-Aging Tea Tree Lip Balm SPF15 inside all of my actor's makeup kits along with a tube in my purse, in my car, and on my nightstand. I need healing too!

### #29 One Moisturizer That's All

Pure aloe makes the perfect all-purpose moisturizer for film and photo. It is oil-free so you're not using more powder than necessary and can be used on even the most sensitive skin.

### #30 Spa Soothing

One of my favorite tools found inside my makeup trailer is my heated towel caddy wafting with aromatherapy scents. I create an essential oil concoction and pour it over wet facial towels. They bake in the caddy (or heat in your microwave) until I use them at wrap time to remove my actor's makeup and treat their skin. Be aware of sensitivities, allergies, contraindications, or proclivities.

### #31 Ready, Aim, Go

Add a smidgen of hand lotion to tame and magically make any wispy flyaway hair behave with just your touch.

### #32 Make Me Blush

There are no rules to your flush—even applying onto your forehead, the tip of your nose, or on your neck can be a motive to balance, lift, contour, and soften the face. To make your forehead look smaller, use a darker color to create the illusion of it being smaller. Dip your brush into loose face powder, tap off excess, and then dip into desired blush product. This helps the color not to grab onto the skin and allows for blend-ability. For a quick eye shadow, apply onto your eyelids. Use a cream blush for dryer skin types, or for if you want that fresh dewy look. You can also layer using both cream and dry blush. If you have a round face with full cheeks like Jennifer Lawrence or Emma Stone, apply your blush a little bit lower than your cheeky apples. For square-shaped faces like Demi Moore, focus your color closer to your nose, the apples of the cheeks, and lightly blend towards the hairline and even towards the brow. This technique will offset the strong jawline. If you have an oval face like Salma Hayek or Angelina Jolie, start the pigment in the middle of the cheek and blend at an upward angle towards your ear. The trick is to establish more width. For heart-shaped faces like Halle Berry's, start below the apple of the cheek (using most of the product here) and create a blended "C" shape toward the hairline up through the temple. To eliminate the purchasing of a collection of blush colors, apply a dab of your matte lip color onto the apple of your cheek and blend. This will tie the colors together.

### #33 Gobble, Gobble

Wish your jawline looked younger, tighter, and straighter? Take a darker powder or cream and apply under chin and jaw. Blend with a sponge. This creates the illusion of a natural shadow versus a turkey neck.

### #34 Take Cover

Always use your concealer last. Apply all other makeup including your foundation, brows, and eyes. Remove any imperfections, smudges, or mistakes with the finish of concealer. You can save product and time.

### #35 Minor Adjustment

Use chocolate brown powder or cream on the tip of the nose and nostrils to create the natural illusion of a shadow and to make your nose appear smaller.

### #36 Lime in the Coconut

Use coconut oil to condition your lashes. Works great to treat dry, brittle lashes (just don't get it in your eyes). Leave out the lime.

### #37 Curly Cue

Curl your lashes with an effect similar to a curling iron. Blow warm air with your blow-dryer onto the lash curler (black spongy piece) until it heats up. Let it cool slightly and test on the back of your hand so it won't burn you. For stick-straight lashes, tilt the curler up and use waterproof mascara to hold the curl. An alternative is a professional Keratin lash curling and lifting treatment that lasts up to three months.

### #38 Lip lasting
My favorite lip stain is Anastasia Liquid Lipstick. There are 28 stellar matte colors and it's long-wearing, waterproof, and smudge-resistant. Wait a few minutes for it to dry and finish with Epicuren's tea tree lip balm for moisture. For regular lipsticks, stain the lip by applying several coats, rub in with Q-tip, finish with loose powder, and blot with tissue.

### #39 Clear Intentions
Powder can be overused and aging. Try using setting spray. Spray at arm's length away for uniformity.

### #40 Silver Spoon
Place a spoon face down over your eyelid while applying mascara to protect your eye shadow from smudges. The spoon also creates leverage to coat and separate each lash.

### #41 Dig Deep
Looking for an intense moisturizing night treatment? I use the Aquafor brand. It's inexpensive and my feet, hands, and elbows love me for days.

### #42 Youthfulness
Applying sunscreen to exposed skin during exterior shots is a priority to keep my actors' continuity correct. Use sunscreen before makeup application or mix with foundation to minimize the effects of aging, and don't forget the back of your hands, ears, and neck. Use fresh sunscreen (not expired, or stored in the heat) for maximum effectiveness, which shouldn't be a problem if used daily.

### #43 Peace, Love, and Makeup

Choosing and applying concealer is essential in perfecting a flawless makeup. Use a creamy concealer for dry skin, heavily pigmented for corrective, and make sure the shade hides imperfections (if it's too light it will highlight instead). To disguise blue undertones, use a pink base to cancel color. Only use concealer on darker areas around the eye where needed like tear troughs, depressions, or hollowing. Press into pores, layer to build coverage, and blend with a damp sponge. Sometimes I use several concealers. It's a magician wrap.

### #44 Agelessness

Laughing makes you younger, or at least that's what I'm counting on. Smile: it's the best makeup a woman can wear.

*Learn more at*
## *www.tristajordan.com*

# Glossary

As in any professional occupation, there are words used with special meanings, like a secret language.

These are common words used behind the scenes over the walkies.

**10-1:** Going to the bathroom.

**10-Twosy:** Going to the bathroom, going to take a little longer.

**10-4:** I understand the information.

**20:** Your location. "What's your 20?"

**Copy:** I got your info and I understand.

**Eyes on:** Can you spot a person or object? "Anyone have eyes on Trista?"

**Flying in:** When that person or object is on the way.

**Go for:** A call or response for someone on the radio.

**Radio check:** A shout out to make sure your radio is working.

**Good check:** When another crew member hears you.

**Stand by:** Used to let another know you will respond momentarily.

**Walkie check:** Same as a radio check.

**Abby Singer:** Second-to-last shot of the day. Named for a crew member who would always alert his crew of the second-to-last shot of a setup, scene, or the day.

**Apple:** A solid wooden box. The largest size is a full apple, then on down to half, quarter, or pancake apple.

**Back in:** A phrase meaning lunch or break is over and work has started.

**C47:** A clothespin.

**Crafty:** Craft services area and/or person in charge of craft services.

**C-Stand:** A metal pole used to stabilize lights and flags.

**Day Player:** A crew member hired for only one day or a handful of days' worth of work.

**Furnie Blanket:** A furniture blanket or sound blanket.

**Gary Coleman:** A small C-stand.

**Hot Points:** Yelled when carrying something with the potential to hit somebody, such as a dolly track or a C-stand. Usually said when going through a narrow hallway, doorway, or around a corner.

**Juicer:** An electrician.

**Last Looks:** A phrase to call in hair/makeup/wardrobe to give a final touch-up to actors before a scene is filmed. Duh...you read my book?

**Last Man:** A phrase that refers to the last person to get their food at lunch; usually used because lunch should not start until the last man has gone through.

**Magic Hour:** The time right before sunrise/after sunset when the sky is somewhat dark but still illuminated. Often lasts only 20 minutes, despite its name.

**Marsha:** Like the famous words in the *Brady Bunch* sitcom, "Marsha, Marsha, Marsha." It's the third-to-the-last setup, scene, or shot of the day.

**Martini:** The last shot of the day.

**Outtake:** A scene or portion of work removed in the editing process and not included in the final version.

**Pancake:** A size of apple box; see "Apple."

**Picture's Up:** A phrase to alert all on set that cameras are almost set to start rolling.

**Scripty:** The script supervisor.

**Sides:** A half-sized script containing only the scenes being shot that day.

**Sparks:** An electrician; see "Juicer."

**Stinger:** An extension cord.

**Tail lights:** Left the location after wrap.

**Talent:** Actor or actress.

**Video Village:** The area in which viewing monitors are placed for the director and other production personnel. Referred to by this name because of the propensity to fill with people, chairs, and overall "too many cooks in the kitchen."

**Camera Department Terms:**

**1 & 2:** Usually used as shorthand by the director of photography (D.P.) to mean the first mark and the second mark of a camera move.

**Air:** Compressed canned air.

**AKS:** An abbreviation used to refer to a miscellaneous collection of tools or equipment. Stands for "all kinds of stuff."

**Babies or baby sticks:** Small tripod legs.

**Chammy or Shammy:** An eyepiece chamois used to cover the eyecup of the viewfinder; made of cloth or animal skin.

**Crossing:** Phrase used to inform the camera operator when you walk in front of the lens.

**Dirt:** A sand bag.

**Ditty:** Refers to a tool bag with camera lenses used to store the essentials for a camera assistant.

**Dumb Side:** Looking in the same direction as the lens, the right side of the camera.

**Dutch:** To tilt the camera diagonally at a canted angle.

**EVF:** Electronic View Finder.

**Gaff:** Gaffer's tape.

**Hard Tape:** A metal tape measure.

**Jam:** To sync, usually time code.

**M.O.S.:** To shoot without any sound being recorded; refers to Minus Optical Strip (or sound).

**Port cap:** The cover for the lens hole on a camera.

**QRP:** Quick release plate.

**Sand:** A sand bag.

**Second Sticks:** A call made by/to inform the second assistant camera (AC) that the clap of the slate sticks was not properly captured the first time and is needed again.

**Sharps:** Focus, used as a noun.

**Smart Side:** Looking in the same direction as the lens, the left side of the camera.

**Softie:** The first AC or focus puller.

**Soft Tape:** A cloth tape measure.

**Tap:** The monitor or viewing system connected to the camera.

**T-Stops:** Similar to f-stops, t-stops are the measurement of light coming into the lens while compensating the amount of light lost within the lens.

# Tristinary

A bit of silliness with my own made-up words.

**Chocolate chippies:** Moles.

**Cubaconfusa:** The art of completely confusing the confused, like what I did with Cuba Gooding Jr.

**Dotkin:** Daughter.

**DotDot:** Granddaughter

**Ear jam:** Sticky earwax.

**Eye cookies:** Crusty little bits inside the corners of your eyes.

**FINE:** Freakishly inadequately neurotically expressive.

**Foggy Noggin:** Anyone exhibiting clueless or catatonic behavior.

**Nose Pops:** A technique used with hot wax and a popsicle stick to remove unwanted hair inside the nostrils.

**LYM:** Love you massive.

**UMS:** Ugly Mood Swing (men-only, because women have PMS).

**Waswife:** Woman who is now your ex.

**Wasband:** Male who is now your ex.

# In Memoriam

Asa Ropp
Brittany Murphy
Garry Marshall
Craig Thomas
Michael Thomas
Steve Thomas
Michael Woods
Robert Heiman

*Please leave me a review on www.Amazon.com*
*And that's a wrap. Fade to black.*